Selection of Library Materials for Area Studies

Part II. Australia, Canada, and New Zealand

Cecily Johns
Editor

William Z. Schenck
Assistant Editor

Collection Management and Development Committee
Association for Library Collections
and Technical Services

AMERICAN LIBRARY ASSOCIATION · CHICAGO and LONDON · 1994

Maps courtesy of Davis Zvejnieks, University of Toronto Library

Cover and text design by Harriett Banner

Composed by Publishing Services, Inc., Bettendorf, Iowa in Sabon on Xyvision/Linotype L330

Printed on 50-pound Glatfelter, a pH-neutral stock, and bound in 10-point C1S cover stock by McNaughton-Gunn, Inc.

The paper used in this publication meets the minimum requirements of American National Standard for Information Sciences—Permanence of Paper for Printed Library Materials, ANSI Z39.48-1984. ∞

Library of Congress Cataloging-in-Publication Data

Selection of library materials for area studies.
    "Collection Management and Development Committee, Association for Library Collections and Technical Services, American Library Association."
    Includes bibliographical references and index.
    Contents: pt. 1. Asia, Iberia, the Caribbean, and Latin America, Eastern Europe and the Soviet Union, and the South Pacific — pt. 2. Australia, Canada, and New Zealand.
    1. Libraries—Special collections—Area studies. 2. Area studies—Bibliography—Methodology. 3. Selection of nonbook materials. 4. Book selection. I. Johns, Cecily. II. Association for Library Collections & Technical Services. Collection Management and Development Committee.
Z688.A68S44   1990   025.2′9   89-18502
ISBN 0-8389-0528-5 (pt. 1)
ISBN 0-8389-0631-1 (pt. 2)

Printed in the United States of America.
98 97 96 95 94   5 4 3 2 1

Contents

Preface

Three years ago *Selection of Library Materials for Area Studies,* Part I, was published. That volume covered Asia, Iberia, the Caribbean and Latin America, Eastern Europe and the Soviet Union, and the South Pacific. Plans were to include Africa, the Middle East, Western Europe, New Zealand, and Australia in a later volume. Since that time the Collection Management and Development Section of ALCTS decided that to exclude Canada would be a mistake, especially since so many research libraries were developing Canadiana collections. So the concept of publishing a volume that would cover selection strategies for the three Commonwealth countries, Canada, Australia, and New Zealand, was conceived.

As in the earlier volume on Area Studies, the emphasis here is on strategies for gathering and providing comprehensive coverage of the publication output of these regions rather than on careful selection. What makes this volume distinctive among the Area Studies volumes is that the bibliographic structure of these countries is extensive. Strategies described in this volume are more traditional, following models for selecting English language materials published in the United States. Nevertheless, the essays provide unique information about the most useful bibliographic sources, how to identify and acquire publications in languages other than English, specialties of major book dealers, and publication patterns unique to these countries.

Once again I want to thank individuals from the Collection Management and Development Section of ALCTS for their support and advice about this project, especially Anna Perrault, past chair of the Publications and Publicity Committee, and David Farrell, past chair of the Collection Management and Development Section.

CECILY JOHNS

v

Part II

AUSTRALIA, CANADA, AND NEW ZEALAND

INTRODUCTION

William Z. Schenck

These three essays comprise the second volume of *Selection of Library Materials for Area Studies*. Covering Australia, New Zealand, and Canada, these essays provide practical advice on selection tools as well as valuable background information on the history, culture, and current state of publishing in these nations. They are aimed at the generalists who must make intelligent selection decisions and they provide in-depth information for those needing to build larger or more specialized collections. While not all areas of publication and scholarship are covered in depth, the books and journals mentioned provide access to more specialized sources of information.

The reader may well ask why these three widely separated nations are grouped together in this volume. The easy answer is that the three are grouped together because they don't fit elsewhere. Australia and New Zealand, for example, are geographically part of Asia but have had little in common (at least until the last decade) with the nations of East and Southeast Asia. Culturally, politically, ethnically, and economically, these two antipodean nations are much closer to Europe in general and Great Britain in particular.

But a closer examination shows these nations have more than just a common language, membership in the British Commonwealth, and allegiance to the British monarch. The three share a common political system inherited from Great Britain. Economically they are part of the growing Pacific Rim community of trading partners. Culturally they share a language and to some extent a literary heritage and history. Their publishing, book distribution, and educational systems are similar, based on a British model but modified to meet local needs. All these factors make it logical to group these three nations together in this volume.

Traditionally libraries have acquired materials published in Europe, Asia, and third world countries in order to support academic programs or, in the case of public libraries, to provide reading for ethnic populations they serve. Canadian studies flourish at a small number of American colleges and universities; a smaller number have or are planning Australian studies programs. But the reasons for acquiring publications from Canada, Australia, and New Zealand transcend the need to support specialized area study programs.

The three countries face many of the same issues and problems affecting contemporary American society. Australia, New Zealand, and Canada, like the United States, are discussing, arguing, and writing about issues such as the role of minorities in society, multiculturalism, diversity, the role of women, the effect of the frontier on society, the environment, health care, and trade and protectionism, to list just a few. While these issues are not unique to these nations, their similarities and relationships to American culture and society make their experiences, options, and solutions of value to Americans. The increasing availability of information, expanded indexing and abstracting services, Internet connections to library catalogs, and ease of communications among scholars worldwide all support a globalization of resources. The fact that the majority of publishing in these three countries is in the English language increases readership for Americans.

Some works published in these nations, especially fiction by prominent authors, are easily available in the United States through co-publication or distribution arrangements. These works tend to be routinely acquired by American libraries as they are often reviewed in the journals used by librarians for selection. However, the titles available here tend to be those that are commercially viable. Thus fiction by lesser-known writers, literary criticism, and most non-fiction titles are not likely to be available.

The reader will find striking similarities in the publishing scenes. All three areas were deeply affected by the mergers in the publishing world in the 1980s. One result in all three nations (as it has also been in the United States) is the rise of the small specialty press producing high quality and scholarly works. There has also been an increase in (and publishing houses devoted to) books on ethnic and women's issues or fiction published by non-mainstream writers and alternative press publications.

Privatization is a major factor in government publishing in Australia and New Zealand, especially in the scientific and technical field, as governments (at both the state and federal level) have cut expenditures. As a result, it is becoming more difficult for librarians to identify and acquire works in the pure and applied sciences from these nations.

Even with such impediments, publications useful to American scholars, students, policy-makers, and the general public can be identified and acquired from Canada, Australia, and New Zealand with little investment of additional time or skill. This investment is worthwhile, one that will reap the benefit of better scholarship and a more global perspective on issues facing America.

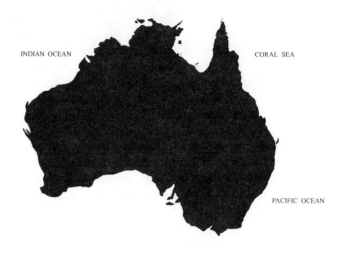

AUSTRALIA

William Z. Schenck

Crocodile Dundee. The Outback. The Sydney Opera House. These are popular images of Australia in the American mind. And while these may be simplistic, they are representative of the diversity of this antipodal continent. In the last two decades, Australian movies have provided Americans with an insight into Australian culture. The American view of the outback has contributed to our romantic view of Australia, while the Sydney Opera House is a symbol of the arts in Australia. These and other images and events, especially Australia's bicentennial in 1988 and its hosting of the Olympics in the year 2000, have generated an increased interest in things Australian.

American academic libraries acquire Australian materials, not only to support Australian studies nor just to provide the Australian perspective on specific issues, but to acquire materials that support research itself. Many of the issues prominent in Australian publishing are the same issues being debated and discussed in the United States. Researchers and students interested in topics such as the environment, race relations, the ozone layer, and the development of a multicultural society will find valuable work being done in Australia. Public libraries acquire contemporary Australian fiction, including titles by such popular mystery writers as Peter Corris and Arthur Upfield and more classical works popularized in this country by such movies as *The Man from Snowy River* and *My Brilliant Career.*

There has been a major increase in interest in Australia in the United States in the last ten years, due in part to cultural reasons, but also to economic reasons. United States and Australian economic ties have always been strong, but after the changes in the 1980s, when Asia became our dominant trading partner, Australia has taken on increased importance. Australia is now the United States' thirteenth largest trading partner; the United States is Australia's second largest trading partner.

The major centers for Australian studies in the United States are at Pennsylvania State University (P.S.U.) and the University of Texas at Austin. The Australian-New Zealand Studies Center at Pennsylvania State had its origins in the 1940s when a course in Australian literature was first given in 1942. The materials collected to support that course and faculty research gave P.S.U. an excellent collection of Australian and New Zealand literature. Published catalogs by Sutherland and Albinski describe the collections.[1] Other strong collections are in the Library of Congress, Yale University, the University of Oregon, and the University of Iowa. The University of Texas founded the Edward A. Clark Center for Australian Studies in 1988. Supported by the collections of the general libraries and especially those of the Harry Ransom Humanities Research Center, this special collection is described in *Perspectives on Australia.*[2]

Nan Bowman Albinski has recently compiled the first directory of Australian collections in American and Canadian libraries. This guide identifies collections, large and small, by reporting institutions. This publication, *Directory of Resources for Australian Studies in North America,* is available for $15 (plus $2 postage) from the Australian-New Zealand Studies Center, Pennsylvania State University, 422 Boucke Building, University Park, PA 16802.[3] This is the first specialized guide to such collections. A similar guide of Australian and New Zealand collections in Great Britain was compiled by Valerie Bloomfield.[4]

The 1980s saw, if not an explosion, at least a heightened awareness of Australia. Several new journals started, including *Australia and New Zealand Studies in Canada* and *The Australian and New Zealand Journal of Serials Librarianship.* (This latter journal has not only articles about serials librarianship, but also subject-based articles such as science-fiction journals in Australia.) The Australian Studies Discussion Group, part of the Association of College and Research Libraries of the American Library Association (ALA), was founded in 1987. This group meets at the semi-annual ALA meetings to discuss developments relating to Australia, New Zealand, and the islands of the western Pacific. A newsletter, containing information on the agenda for the ALA meeting, plus items and notes of interest, is published twice a year and sent free to interested librarians.

Probably the major event of the 1980s was the founding of the American Association of Australian Literary Studies (AAALS) in 1986. Its journal, *Antipodes,* published twice a year, contains articles, works of fiction, reviews of current Australian literary works, and an annual bibliography of literary works and criticism.

There is a popular component to the academic interest in Australia. Popular literature of Australia has been widely reviewed in popular journals and newspapers. An article in the *Washington Post Book World* in 1988 reported that the Australian Literary Council counted eighty-eight recent reviews of Australian books in American newspapers and magazines. Supported by grants, several Australian poets and authors toured the United States in the 1980s, giving interviews and reading from works in progress.[5]

History and Geography

Much of what happens in Australia today is a direct result of its history and geography. Aborigines, the first people to inhabit Australia, came to Australia from Asia somewhere between 40,000 and 70,000 years ago. They developed a complex, nomadic culture, much of which was destroyed through European conquest or disease. European discovery of the continent came in the seventeenth century; Captain James Cook claimed possession of the continent for England in 1770. After the American Revolution, Britain had to find new penal colonies and, looking to Australia, sent a fleet of eleven ships with 1,530 people, including 736 convicts, to establish the first colony in 1788 near the site of what is now Sydney. (The settlement of Australia is best told in *The Fatal Shore,* by Robert Hughes.[6])

The environment of Australia has always determined settlements. By the middle of the nineteenth century, settlements had been established in most of the coastal areas, but the inhospitable nature of the interior blocked settlement beyond the coast. Immigration continued throughout the nineteenth century, at times accelerated by specific events such as the gold rushes between 1851 and 1860 that attracted over 600,000 settlers to Australia.

While Australia is the sixth largest country in the world (the size of the United States minus Alaska and West Virginia), it has only about seventeen million people. Most of the population continue to be concentrated in two widely separated coastal regions on the southeast and southwest. Australia is one of the most urban nations in the world, with 71 percent of its population living in centers of 100,000 or more. Just under 40 percent of the population live in the two largest cities, Sydney and Melbourne.

In the nineteenth and early part of the twentieth centuries, immigration to Australia was primarily from England and Ireland. But in the 1920s and the 1930s, there was an increase in the number of immigrants from southern Europe. After the Second World War, almost 500,000 people immigrated, about 60 percent of them non-British. After 1956, there was a progressive liberalization of the policy that had restricted the immigration of non-Europeans, and since 1973, Australia has had a specific policy of non-discrimination by race, nationality, and religion. As a result, immigrants are now coming from western Asia, Southeast Asia, and Latin America, rather than from Europe. This has significantly diversified Australia's culture. According to the census of 1966, approximately two million Australians use a language other than English in their homes. The major languages, other than English, are Italian, Greek, Chinese, German, and Arabic. The Australia of the twenty-first century will be truly a multicultural society, a development that will be more and more reflected in its publishing.

Government

The nation of Australia dates to 1901 when the states of New South Wales, Victoria, Queensland, Western Australia, South Australia, and Tasmania formed the Commonwealth of Australia. The Australian government in Canberra is responsible for the matters relating to national interest. The six state governments, plus the Northern Territory and the Australian Capital Territory, have parliamentary governments. As the states have significant powers, publications of state governments, in addition to their official publications, can be important to U.S. libraries.

Publishing

The first book published in Australia was actually a government publication: *New South Wales General Standing Orders,* printed in 1802. But through the entire nineteenth century, most books were imported from the United Kingdom. The majority of the printed books from that century focused on exploration, Australia's fauna and flora, travel, and official reports. It was not until the 1860s that an Australian national spirit began to appear through publishing; in 1886 the firm of Angus & Robertson, Australia's oldest publisher, was founded. "Robertson brought to bear on publishing a skill, a vigor, and a faith in the future of Australian books that surpassed anything that had prevailed up to that time."[7]

The latter half of the nineteenth century saw the beginning of Australian literature, with authors such as Andrew Barton "Banjo" Paterson, Mary Gilmore, Henry Handel Richardson, and Henry Lawson. This was the period of the bush ballad and tales of individuals and life in Australia's inhospitable outback. Many late nineteenth-century titles have recently been reprinted, often with scholarly introductions, and are easily acquired.

Australia's writers, even in the nineteenth century, faced the problem of competition from English and American writers who were more established and promoted by the literary establishment. Even authors as popular as Henry Lawson felt this inferiority:

> The Australian writer, until he gets a "London hearing," is only accepted as an imitator of some recognized English or American author; and, as soon as he shows signs of coming to the front he is labelled "The Australian Southey," "The Australian Burns," or "The Australian Bret Harte," and, "The Australian Kipling." Thus, no matter how original he may be, he is branded, at the very start, as a plagiarist.[8]

There was a small increase in Australian publishing in the period after the First World War, but many of its literary authors, including Miles Franklin, Norman Lindsay, Eleanor Dark, and Vance Palmer, still had to find publishers in London for their works, although Angus & Robertson continued to publish Australian writers. Before World War II, Australia's writers began to establish a more distinctive Australian literature, but it was not until after the war, when population grew and educational levels rose, that there was a great increase in publishing in Australia. Although the Melbourne University Press had been established in 1922, other university presses, including The University of Western Australia Press, University of Queensland Press, University of New South Wales Press, and the Australian National University Press, were established between 1948 and 1966. Australia's major literary magazines, *Meanjin, Quadrant, Westerly,* and *Overland,* were founded and major Australian writers such as Alec Derwent Hope, Thomas Keneally, and Patrick White gained international reputations. However, even between 1945 and 1980, "the value of books imported from Britain and America is four times the value of books published . . . in Australia."[9] By 1987, imports had decreased to only half the books sold in Australia. U.S. and English publishers opened branches in Australia. During the 1980s works by many Australian writers were available in the U.S. market, either through American editions of their works or by distribution of Australian editions. Librarians ordering Australian books should first check *Books in Print* to determine if the books are available in the United States.

By the second half of the 1980s, publishing had consolidated. The Australian publishing industry has been as affected as its American and British counterparts by mergers, takeovers, and personnel changes. However, the consolidation often had the opposite effect as editors left large firms to start new publishing companies. Thus, a feature of Australian publishing in the 1980s, not unlike that in the United States, was the proliferation of small presses, including Wild and Wooley, known for its alternative political works; Currency Press, a publisher of Australian plays; and the Fremantle Arts Centre Press, known for its art and works relating to Western Australia.

Book Publishing Statistics

It is difficult to obtain accurate statistics on the number of items published each year and impossible to know how many of these would be of value to American libraries. In 1989, the *Australian National Bibliography* listed 9,759 books and pamphlets, but this figure includes only items cataloged by Australian libraries and not the total output of Australian publishers.

The annual cumulative edition of the *Australian National Bibliography* contains statistics on publishing in Australia over the past ten years. Commercial publishing peaked in 1987 when 4,067 books were issued; it dropped to 3,879 in 1989, the most recent complete year available. Approximately the same number of titles from societies and institutions was published in these years, while there has been a small decline in the number of books published by the state and national governments, from a high of 3,561 in 1984 to 2,240 in 1989. There are approximately 4,000 serials published in Australia. English is the predominant language of publishing, although there has been a small increase in non-English-language publishing.

The major publishers' association in Australia is the Australian Book Publishers' Association (ABPA), representing over 150 commercial publishers. An excellent overview of Australian publishing is the annual *Australian Book Scene*. Published as a supplement to the *Australian Bookseller and Publisher,* it is most easily attained from the Australian book suppliers listed at the end of this article. The *Australian Book Scene* provides profiles of a cross section of Australian publishers, a list of major Australian literary award winners, and brief reviews of recent Australian books. It also lists addresses of selected publishers.

Governments, both state and national, are also major publishers in Australia. The Australian Government Publishing Service (AGPS) was established in 1970 to consolidate and promote government publishing. AGPS publications are often scholarly works on topics or issues of importance to Americans. Other major publishers of government information are the Australian Broadcasting Corporation, the National Library of Australia, the Australian War Museum, and, for scientific and technical works, the Commonwealth Scientific and Industrial Research Organization (CSIRO). Since government publishing has been affected by budget cuts and the worldwide movement toward privatization, librarians must expect to pay more for these publications and may find exchange programs less efficient as a method of acquisition.

Reference

Murray Martin's article, "An Australian Reference Collection for College Libraries," in *Choice* (January, 1988) provides a good summary of available reference works. The *Oxford Companion to Australian Literature* provides an excellent summary, not just of major authors, but also of works and writers important to historical and cultural events. Of special value are the essays on "Aboriginal in Australian Literature" and "Feminism and Australian Literature." Ken Goodwin's *A History of Australian Literature* is a good, general survey of literature in Australia.

Selection

The challenge faced by librarians is to learn what is available and to find a source that can provide the item on a timely basis. Overall, bibliographical control of Australian publications is excellent. Librarians acquiring materials only in specific areas (e.g., wine making, arid lands studies) will have a relatively easy time as they will need to look in just one or two sources, while the librarian acquiring materials of a general nature will need to use several sources.

A recent publication, *Australian Studies: Acquisitions and Collection Development for Libraries,* provides a good, general overview of publishing in Australia.[10] Of special value is the essay by Ross Atkinson, "Developing an Australian Literature Collection: An American Perspective." This essay provides an excellent model for developing a literature collection; it is also an excellent guide to current sources on Australian literature.

There are two major factors that inhibit the acquisition of Australian books. The first is distance; the second is the overall Australian attitude toward business.

The tyranny of distance makes communications difficult, even in these days of electronic mail and fax. Travel to Australia is expensive and the distance between centers of publishing and scholarship discourages the library traveler. This is partly compensated for by the number of Australian librarians and faculty who visit American colleges and universities on a regular basis. Librarians interested in current developments in Australia should talk with visiting Australians.

The unresponsiveness of some (but not all) Australian publishers can be frustrating to the American librarian. An entertaining view of doing business in Australia is shown in the movie *The Coca-Cola Kid* (available in video). The Australian government does not actively promote Australian books outside Australia, and funds available to the Australian Embassy and its consulates to support cultural activities and book donation programs have decreased in recent years.

Selection Tools—Current

An approval plan is the most effective method to use to acquire new Australian titles for those libraries with broad collecting interests. Both of the two Australian book dealers, Bennett and Walshe, offer such plans, and both also provide a slip service to notify librarians of new titles.

The *Australian National Bibliography (ANB)*, compiled and published by the National Library of Australia, is the most comprehensive selection tool available. It is published monthly, with quarterly and annual cumulations. The *ANB* lists books and pamphlets, including government publications, published in Australia in the current and preceding two years. The *ANB* contains books cataloged by the National Library and by libraries that are part of the Australian Bibliography Network. New serials are also listed in the *ANB*. Citations, with full bibliographical information, are arranged according to the Dewey decimal classification. Price is given, in Australian dollars, when available. The *ANB* contains author, title, and series indexes. The major advantage of the *ANB* is its comprehensiveness; the disadvantage, for selection, is its neutrality; like any national bibliography, it is just a listing of titles. Bibliographical records from the *ANB* will soon be available on OCLC and RLIN.

The Guide to New Australian Books, published bimonthly, started publishing in 1990. It gives brief reviews (about fifty words each) of new Australian books. The reviews are arranged by title, with a subject and author index. The annotations, primarily descriptive and not critical, are prepared by staff of the National Center for Australian Studies at Monash University. The emphasis is on popular books, but some scholarly works are included. The advantage of the *GNAB* is the extensive coverage (about five hundred books per issue) and descriptions; the disadvantage of the journal is the lack of any critical commentary.

Selection Tools—Evaluative

In addition to the sources listed above, there are some excellent review sources that can be used for more selective acquisitions or for monitoring other selection sources. Of these, the best is the National Library's

Australian Books (AB). It has been published annually since 1933 (until 1948 its title was *Select List of Representative Works Dealing with Australia*). *AB* "is designed as a current reference and reading list of works dealing with Australia or by Australian authorship which, in the opinion of librarians and book reviewers, are authoritative or of outstanding quality." Books are grouped by general subjects. Recommended general works still in print are listed, plus selected works on the subjects recently published. The emphasis of books listed is not scholarly, but on books of interest to the general layperson. The 1991 *AB* included about seven hundred books. *AB* is an excellent source, especially for librarians wanting to acquire basic works on a subject.

Two annual bibliographies are also valuable for evaluation. The "Annual Bibliography of Studies in Australian Literature" is published in the annual *Australian Literature Studies*. It is particularly valuable as it lists selected items relating to Australian studies and new books with reviews of contemporary Australian writers. The December issue of *Antipodes* contains the "Bibliography of Australian Literature and Criticism Published in North America," compiled by Nan Bowman Albinski.

The *Australian Book Review (ABR)* is published ten times a year by the National Book Council of Australia. Containing articles on Australian culture and publishing, it provides in-depth reviews of between fifteen and twenty books. While the *ABR* has no specific emphasis, it is a valuable review resource for books of general scholarly, including political, issues.

Several journals provide valuable reviews. *Antipodes,* the journal of the American Association of Australian Literary Studies, is published twice a year and has excellent reviews on Australian literary books. Three Australian quarterly journals, *Meanjin, Overland,* and *Westerly,* all worthwhile additions to American libraries, review new Australian literary works. The *Journal of Australian Studies,* covering interdisciplinary studies of Australian culture, reviews about ten books per issue. *Quadrant,* called by Bill Katz, "the Australian version of *American Scholar,*" is Australia's leading intellectual monthly and its reviews cover a variety of subjects.

The major periodical index in Australia is *APAIS (Australian Public Affairs Information Service: A Subject Index to Current Literature),* compiled and published since 1945 by the National Library. This is also available in a useful CD-ROM called *AUSTROM* that includes entries from 1980 to the present. *APAIS* provides subject access to periodical literature in the humanities and the social sciences. (There is no comparable index in science, as the index *Australian Science Index* ceased publication in 1983.) *APAIS* also indexes books, pamphlets, and conference proceedings that are not covered adequately in the *ANB*. It is also a good source for information on the other, more specialized Australian periodical indexes.

Selection Tools—Specialized

The major scientific publisher in Australia is the Commonwealth Scientific and Industrial Research Organization (CSIRO). CSIRO employs about seven thousand people and supports over one hundred laboratories and field stations. CSIRO publications range from technical reports on specialized areas to general scientific works. Recent moves to require that CSIRO recover costs have meant there is a tendency to publish more applied research. CSIRO publishes *CSIRO Publications*. This annual lists new works, including journals, plus a backlist of titles still in print, with prices. Librarians acquiring CSIRO works on specialized research may want to scan the annual reports of the various CSIRO divisions distributed through normal channels.

Australian Government Publishing Service (AGPS) publishes and distributes the majority of publications from the national government. Each state has its own publishing operation. In recent years there has been a concerted move to make government operations more self sufficient. This was carried to the extreme recently when the government of New South Wales closed its public printer. The overall result has been more emphasis on "commercial" publications to the detriment of more specialized works.

Publications of AGPS are covered in the *Australian National Bibliography*. The National Library publishes *Australian Government Publications (AGP)*, a listing of state and national government publications. *AGP* has been published on microfiche only since March, 1988. It is issued quarterly with annual cumulations. *AGP* contains listings for government publications listed in the *Australian National Bibliography*; it also contains listings for AGPS and CSIRO publications, plus state publications cataloged by either the National Library or any other institution contributing to the National Bibliographic Database.

AGPS catalogs listing their publications plus the publications of the Australian War Memorial, the National Library of Australia, and AUS-LIG (the Australian Survey and Lands Information Group) are the more convenient sources of information about government publications. AGPS publishes several catalogs that are useful for selection. Its *Commonwealth Publications, Official List* is issued fortnightly and includes just the AGPS titles produced in that time period. A more selected list of AGPS and

AGPS-distributed titles can be found in *New Releases from the Australian Government Publishing Service* that began publishing in the first quarter, 1992. AGPS also produces, on microfiche, the *Annual Catalogue of Commonwealth Publications*. Selected AGPS titles are listed in AGPS catalogs of publications for sale in the United States (available from AGPS, P.O. Box 7, Planetarium Station, New York, NY 10023).

The publishing scene for federal, state, and quasi-governmental organizations in Australia is complex and changing. Librarians desiring a more detailed description of government publishing will find the essay by Michael Harrington in Gorman's books to be useful.[11]

The Australian Library Publishers' Society (ALPS) is a consortium of thirty-two Australian libraries, library associations, library schools, and small publishers of library-related materials, formed to make their publications more widely available. The ALPS 1990 catalog lists 283 publications, giving brief descriptions. The items all pertain to Australia; they are often bibliographies or items not likely to be reviewed or available through the commercial book trade. ALPS markets the publications; issuing institutions handle sales.

Books relating to Australian aborigines cross a variety of disciplines. The best collection of materials relating to aborigines is at the Australian Institute of Aboriginal and Torres Strait Islander Studies. Its publishing arm, the Aboriginal Studies Press, issues about twelve titles a year. Since 1966, the AIAS has issued an annual bibliography that covers a wide range of materials. While major works will have appeared in the other selection services described above, the AIAS is a good source for specialized studies.

There is increased interest in Australia in books about nineteenth-century life. Australian presses are either reprinting older texts or publishing diaries and memoirs such as the Colonial Text Series published by the New South Wales University Press. The Mulini Press publishes a catalog called *Australian Nineteenth Century Literature in Print* (ANCLIP). This catalog lists nineteenth-century works available from fifty-one Australian publishers. Works are listed by author, without annotation. It is especially valuable for libraries wishing to purchase works by nineteenth-century Australian writers. Many reprints from small presses that may not otherwise be reviewed are listed.

The increase in immigrants for whom English is a second language has been followed, albeit slowly, with increased writing and publishing in other languages. While some of these writers publish in their native languages, others write for the larger, English-reading audience. The recently published *Bibliography of Australian Multicultural Writers* provides a detailed listing of these authors.[12]

Children's Books

Children's books have always had a high profile in Australian publishing.[13] American libraries wanting to purchase quality children's books should acquire those books winning the three Children's Book Council Awards (Book of the Year for Older Readers, Book of the Year for Younger Readers, and the Picture Book of the Year. These are announced during Children's Book Week in August). Angus & Robertson and Oxford University Press have published excellent children's books. A good source for selection of children's books is the annual list published in *Australian Books.* The new Thorpe publication, *Subject Guide to Australian Children's Books in Print,* lists 3,500 books in 1,800 subjects.

Selection—Retrospective

Most librarians will concentrate on current titles, as it is more difficult, especially for American libraries, to obtain out-of-print books from Australia. Two works by Brian Howes assist American librarians in their retrospective purchases: *Guide to Fine and Rare Australasian Books* and *Antiquarian and Secondhand Book Dealers in Australia.* The former lists seven thousand Australian books offered for sale between 1982 and 1984 by major Australian dealers. Only items costing more than $A40 (about $25 U.S.) are listed. Perusal of the volume provides an overview of prices. The latter volume provides information on dealers who may be helpful to the librarian looking for dealers who specialize in specific subjects.

One of the most effective ways to acquire older Australian books is to obtain catalogs from Australian university presses and other major publishers and then order in-print titles in subjects of interest. Australian book dealers can assist in this.

Literary Awards

The first literary award in Australia was made in 1820 when the governor of New South Wales awarded Michael Massey Robinson two cows for his service as the Antipodean Poet Laureate. The tradition of government support continues today, and one writer has even suggested that "every current Australian novel is preceded by a grant and followed by a prize."[14] However, the amount of money the government provides for writers has decreased in recent years. Selecting prize-winning books is a good way to build a quality collection of Australiana. Major awards are listed each year in the *Australian Book Scene*. Major awards are the Miles Franklin Award, the *Age* Book of the Year Award, and, for children's books, the Children's Book Council Awards (see listing above). A complete list is available in *Australian Literary Awards and Fellowships*.

Directories

The following directories are useful in acquiring Australian books and serials. Published by Thorpe, they are available from Bowker Reed.

Australian Books in Print is an annual listing that attempts to list available titles from all Australian publishers. Books are listed by author and by title.

Australian Periodicals in Print lists serials (except government publications) published in Australia. Periodicals are listed by publisher, title, and subject.

Australian and New Zealand Booksellers and Publishers can be useful for locating addresses of publishers. The publisher's area of specialty is listed when supplied by the publisher.

Dealers

There are few dealers in Australia established to sell books to American libraries. Both James Bennett and B. H. Walshe will supply Australian books; Bennett-EBSCO (not connected to James Bennett) will supply periodicals. Other U.S. subscription agents can also supply Australian periodicals.

International Specialized Book Services (ISBS) is the U.S. distributor for publications of the Australian Government Publishing Service. ISBS also distributes some publications of CSIRO and several other Australian publishers, including the University of Queensland Press. The Australian Book Source in California and Koala Books in Alberta stock a limited number of Australian books, with emphasis on popular titles. The list of publishers whose books ISBS distributes is subject to change. The Australian Book Source and ISBS issue catalogs but these dealers can obtain titles from Australia. The three North American dealers can be especially helpful when a book title is needed quickly.

Newspapers

Libraries wishing to have current information on Australia should consider a subscription to the *Age,* published in Melbourne, or the *Sydney*

Morning Herald. Both are considered "national" papers. The *Financial Review* provides business and economic information.

Conclusion

To summarize, both popular and research works from Australia are of value to American libraries. While many new Australian titles are distributed in the United States, reliance on this alone will not provide adequate coverage for other than the smallest libraries. Libraries wanting to acquire selectively can use the journals listed in the article plus the annual review *Australian Books*. Libraries collecting more comprehensively should use an approval plan combined with monitoring through the use of the other selection sources described. Government documents, many distributed in the United States, are also an important resource.

Appendix A. Selection Sources

APAIS: Australian Public Affairs Information Service. v. 1– . 1945– . Canberra: National Library of Australia. Monthly.

Antipodes: A North American Journal of Australian Literature. v. 1– . 1987– . New York: American Association of Australian Literature Studies. 2/yr.

Australian and New Zealand Booksellers and Publishers. v. 1– . 1990– . Melbourne: D. W. Thorpe.

Australian Book Review. Melbourne: National Book Council. 10/yr.

Australian Book Scene. v. 1– . 1977– . Melbourne: D. W. Thorpe. Annually.

Australian Books. A Select List of Recent Publications and Standard Works in Print. v. 1– . 1933– . Canberra: National Library of Australia. Annually.

Australian Books in Print. Melbourne: D. W. Thorpe. Annually.

Australian Library Publishers' Society. *Catalogue of Members' Publications*. Adelaide: ALPS, 1990. (Available from Barr Smith Library, P.O. Box 498, 6.P.O. Adelaide, Australia 5001)

Australian Literary Awards and Fellowships. Melbourne: D. W. Thorpe, 1991.

Australian National Bibliography. v. 1– . 1961– . Canberra: National Library of Australia. Monthly.

Australian Nineteenth Century Literature in Print. Jamison Centre: Mulini Press, 1991. (Available from A.N.C.L.I.P., P.O. Box 82, Jamison Centre, ACT, 2614)

Australian Periodicals in Print. v. 1– . 1981– . Melbourne: D. W. Thorpe. Annually.

Australian Studies Discussion Group Newsletter. Austin: ASDG. (Available from Cheryl Knott Malone, PCL 2.430, The General Libraries, The University of Texas, Austin, TX 78713-7330)

Goodwin, Ken. *A History of Australian Literature*. Macmillan History of Literature. London: Macmillan, 1980.

Guide to New Australian Books. v. 1– . 1990– . Melbourne: D. W. Thorpe. 6/yr.

Howes, Brian R. *Antiquarian and Secondhand Book Dealers in Australia: A Directory.* Wagga Wagga: Magpie Books, 1987.

—— *Guide to Fine and Rare Australasian Books.* Wagga Wagga: The Author, 1986. (Available from the Author, P.O. Box 82, Wagga Wagga, NSW 2650.) Volume 3 of the *Guide to Fine and Rare Australasian Books* is available from Magpie Books, 111 Murray Street, Angaston, SA 5353.

Martin Murray S. "An Australian Reference Collection for College Libraries." *Choice,* January, 1988, pp. 735–38.

Wilde, William H., Joy Hooton, and Barry Andrews, eds. *The Oxford Companion to Australian Literature.* Melbourne: Oxford University Press, 1985.

Appendix B. Book Dealers

AUSTRALIAN

Bennett-EBSCO Subscription Service
35 Mitchell St.
North Sydney, NSW 2060
Phone: 02-922-5600
(for periodicals only)

James Bennett Library Service
4 Collaroy St.
Collaroy 1097
Phone: 02-982-2122
Fax: 02-971-1309

B. H. Walshe & Sons
7 Lewis St.
Coburg, Victoria 3058
Phone: 03-350-3722
Fax: 03-350-6624

NORTH AMERICAN SOURCES

Australian Book Source
Susan Curry
1309 Redwood Lane
Davis, CA 95616
Phone: 916-753-1519
Fax: 916-753-6491

International Specialized Book Services (ISBS)
5302 NE Hassalo St.
Portland, OR 97213
Phone: 800-547-7734
Fax: 503-284-8859

Koala Books of Canada
John Carolan
14327-95A Ave.
Edmonton, Alberta
Canada T5N 0B6
Phone and Fax: 403-452-5149

Notes

1. Bruce Sutherland, *Australiana in the Pennsylvania State University Libraries,* Bibliographical Series No. 1 (University Park: Pennsylvania State University Libraries, 1989); Nan Bowman Albinski, *Australian/New Zealand Literature in the Pennsylvania State University Libraries: A Bibliography,* Bibliographical Series No. 11 (University Park: Pennsylvania State University Libraries, 1989).

2. Dave Oliphant, ed., *Perspectives on Australia: Essays on Australiana in the Harry Ransom Humanities Research Center* (Austin: Harry Ransom Humanities Research Center, University of Texas at Austin, 1989).

3. Nan Bowman Albinski, *Directory of Resources for Australian Studies in North America* (University Park: Australian-New Zealand Studies Center, Pennsylvania State University, 1992).
4. Valerie Bloomfield, *Resources for Australian and New Zealand Studies: A Guide to Library Holdings in the United Kingdom* (London: Australian Studies Centre and the British Library, 1986).
5. Valerie Miner, "A Literature of Their Own," *Washington Post Book World,* August 7, 1988, p. 15.
6. Robert Hughes, *The Fatal Shore: The Epic of Australia's Founding* (New York: Random, 1986).
7. John McLaren and Peter Tranter, "Publishing," in *Australian Encyclopedia,* 5th ed. (Sydney: Australian Geographic, 1988), pp. 2421–66.
8. Quoted in Bill Wannan, *Directory of Humorous Australian Quotations and Anecdotes* (Melbourne: Sun Books, 1974), p. 123.
9. Sigfred Taubert, ed., *The Americas, Australia, New Zealand,* Book Trade of the World, v. 2 (Munchen: K. G. Saur, n.d.), p. 347.
10. G. E. Gorman, ed., *Australian Studies: Acquisitions and Collection Development for Libraries* (London: Mansell, 1992).
11. Ibid.
12. *A Bibliography of Australian Multicultural Writers,* comp. Sneja Gunew (Geelong, Victoria: Centre for Studies in Literary Education, Humanities Division, Deakin University, 1992).
13. Robert Sessions, "Children's Book Publishing in Australia: A Lively Business," *Publishers Weekly,* March 24, 1989, pp. 35–37.
14. Miner, p. 15.

NORTH
ATLANTIC

NORTH
PACIFIC

HUDSON
BAY

CANADA

Gayle Garlock

Canada is a culturally diverse country with two official languages and a population spread across a large geographic area. The country has a sophisticated and very active publishing community that is producing a wide range of material available for selection in many different formats. An equally wide range of selection tools exists to be used by the Canadiana selector in developing a collection. An attempt is made here to open up approaches to selecting from all these diverse materials and, of equal importance, approaches to aid selectors in developing their knowledge of Canada and Canadiana.

In developing an effective Canadiana collecting strategy for your institution, the language and geography of the nation have to be taken into consideration. Language coverage should be continually kept in mind in a country with two official languages (English and French) and a multicultural environment where ethnic presses thrive.[1] When evaluating selection aids or reference tools, the question of language coverage always arises and should be addressed if the work in question does not provide good coverage of both English and French publications. The geography of the country also affects the book trade. Because the population is spread out along a narrow belt across the southern boundary of the country, there is an ongoing distribution problem for the trade. On the other hand, this dispersal continues to foster a strong sense of regional identity which, in turn, fosters many smaller, regional publishing houses. Awareness of the strong regional identities and differences, and collecting the publications from the regions will certainly strengthen a collection.

In addition to language and regional coverage, another question to be kept in mind when deciding upon the selection aid(s) to be employed is what definition of Canadiana is used by the works under consideration. Some works, such as the national bibliography *Canadiana,* have an exceptionally broad definition of Canadiana, which includes all works published in Canada, and materials published in foreign countries having Canadian content, or a Canadian connection such as a Canadian author, editor, translator, etc.[2] Other selection tools limit themselves to works published in Canada or a region of Canada. Different types of coverage meet differing collecting needs, and the selection tools chosen should have the coverage that best matches the collection policy of the institution.

History of the Book Trade

ENGLISH

The printing and publishing aspects of the book trade appeared in what is now Canada in the latter half of the eighteenth century. From the beginning, publications in what are now the two official languages of Canada, English and French, began appearing. The first printing press was brought to Halifax from Boston in 1751, and a newspaper was soon produced. In 1764 a press was established in Quebec City, and in 1776 another in Montreal. These cities remained the centers of the nascent Canadian book trade in the eighteenth century with the printer-publishers surviving on government publishing contracts for the most part.

As the explorers and settlers moved westward the economic and publishing center of English language Canada shifted from Halifax to Montreal and then to Toronto in upper Canada. From the beginning Canadian printer-publishers faced the challenges that remain with their modern counterparts. The comparatively small market geographically spread out along the southern boundaries makes distribution difficult and expensive. Added to this was the necessity of competing with much larger American and British publishing companies who had all the advantages of economies of scale. A case in point is that of the popular nineteenth-century Canadian authors Thomas Haliburton and Major John Richardson who found their needs better met by the large British and American publishers and either left (Haliburton) or never published with Canadian firms.

Some firms, however, did manage to succeed. In mid-century the publishing house of John Lovell & Son prospered with quality printing in both languages of newspapers, magazines, directories, government publications, and literary works. Eventually the firm moved to the United States and became a publisher of cheap, paper reprint series. Two other publishers, George Maclean Rose and the Belford Brothers, thrived in Canada during the last quarter of the century through publishing cheap reprints of British and American authors with some of the latter being pirated editions. Another firm, the Methodist Book Publishing House, renamed the Ryerson Press in 1919, first published mainly religious books and then expanded into trade publications in the last two decades of the century to become the most influential Canadian publishing house of the time.

By the end of the nineteenth century many Canadian publishing houses had become exclusive agents for British and American publishers. In other cases new firms had been established that were branch plants for other United States and British publishers. In either case, the agency or the branch plant, the dominance of a foreign publisher has been viewed by many analysts as a force that has worked against the publishing of Canadian authors by these firms. There is some justification for this view, for during this century such Canadian-owned publishing houses as Ryerson, MacMillan, Clarke Irwin, and especially McClelland and Stewart have played a major role in publishing Canadian authors. Before the First World War McClelland and Stewart had published more Canadian authors than all the other Toronto publishers combined. In the twenties Lorne Pierce of Ryerson, Hugh Eayrs of Macmillan, and John McClelland emerged as publishers who were strong advocates of Canadian literature and encouraged the publication of Canadian authors. Following the Great Depression and the Second World War McClelland and Stewart brought out authors such as Irving Layton, Leonard Cohen, Mordecai Richler, Margaret Atwood, and Al Purdy, and in the 1960s the firm brought out the influential Carleton Library Series and the reprint series, New Canadian Library. The 1960s and 1970s also saw a flourishing of new Canadian small presses and regional publishers. Much of this growth can be attributed to the first significant introduction of Canadian literature courses into the educational system in the 1950s and 1960s, and the growth in Canadian studies that emerged after the centennial year of 1967.

The recurring market difficulties of a small market and competition from U.S. and U.K. firms have continued in the 1970s and 1980s. In 1970 the sale of Ryerson to McGraw-Hill (a U.S. firm) along with other factors led to the Ontario Royal Commission on Book Publishing.[3] One recommendation was for funding and loan guarantees for Canadian publishers, and in the 1980s both provincial and federal funds have been made available to support Canadian publishing. However, even the loan guarantees did not save Clarke Irwin, which went into receivership in 1983. In response to concerns over foreign ownership, the federal government established a policy called the Baie-Comeau policy in 1985 designed to increase Canadian control of publishing by restricting foreign ownership of new firms and branch plants acquired through takeovers. The policy has proven costly and ineffective through lack of enforcement, and its future is uncertain in the context of the 1989 free trade agreement with the United States. Recently the financial difficulties for Canadian publishers increased with the federal government's implementation of a goods and services tax, the GST. This tax included books, which previously had not been taxed. In 1991 two more Canadian publishers (Hurtig and Lester, Orpen & Denys) ceased operation.

Currently there is no agreement among the members of the Canadian book trade on solutions for the problems of Canadian publishing. The issues related to foreign ownership are not easily separated from other generic problems of Canadian publishing. The different publishing associations, the booksellers' association, the wholesalers' association, and the library association, endorse differing and sometimes opposing solutions. In the spring of 1992 the federal government proposed changes to the Baie-Comeau policy and has expressed the intent to encourage the various interest groups in the book trade to reach an accord on steps to be taken toward the stabilization of Canadian publishing. These steps will have to address the issue of foreign ownership for English language publishing where the situation is less stable than in Quebec.

Notwithstanding these difficulties Canadian publishers have developed strong lists. Eminent creative writers have gained international recognition with their titles appearing simultaneously in London, New York, and Toronto, and a growing international interest in Canadian studies has also fostered the publication and sales of Canadian books.

FRENCH

When compared to English-Canadian publishing the history of the Quebec French language book trade has interesting differences that have led to an economic environment that encourages the publication of Quebec books. The Quebec book trade had similar beginnings with the usual printer-publisher arrangement for the eighteenth and early stages of the nineteenth century. However, in the nineteenth century the state gave the church responsibility for education, and, in the mid-century, the religious communities took over the production and distribution of textbooks, a process that they continued to control until the 1960s. Meanwhile any secular publishing was being done by the large bookstores such as Beauchemin, Granger, Garneau, Wilson, and LaFleur.

Changes began to be introduced into this long-lived organizational structure with the defeat of France in World War II. Publishers independent of bookstores established themselves in response to the demand for French language publications, and some of them survived the difficult postwar years. Then in the 1960s and 1970s major changes occurred. Concerns about the "crisis" in Quebec bookselling led to the Bouchard Report of 1965. This report set up the framework for a government book policy and indirectly brought about the end of the engagement of religious institutes in publishing. At the same time the threat of foreign ownership was arising as French publishers and agents began to establish themselves in the Quebec market. Hachette in 1968 forced all Quebec bookstores to buy their French books from them and then bought out the Garneau bookstore chain. Steps such as this threatened to eliminate the traditional bookstore distribution system in Quebec. In 1973 the Quebec government passed three laws that stipulated that all provincially subsidized institutions, e.g., schools, universities, public libraries, and the government itself, must buy Quebec and foreign books from accredited bookstores. Bookstores could only be accredited if at least 51 percent of the ownership was held by Quebec residents. In effect the earlier control by religious societies was replaced by government regulations that were intended to encourage Quebec ownership of the publishing and distributions systems. As a result of these laws and federal and provincial funding, Quebec publishing grew very rapidly. For example, in 1968 Quebec publishers produced 819 titles whereas 3,997 titles appeared in 1977. Notwithstanding the ongoing problems of a limited marketplace, the result has been a much stronger, stabilized provincial book trade.

Contemporary Book Trade

A working knowledge of the Canadian book trade constitutes one of the essential requirements of a good Canadiana selector. One should know the major publishers and the characteristics of their lists, know how the distribution system works, and be aware of the roles the government plays in the book trade from grants to taxes. The acquisition of all this and other knowledge contributes to the formation of an informed selector who can make meaningful contributions toward the development of the collection.

A current overview of the size of Canadian publishing can be gained from government statistics. In 1990–91, 314 publishers with annual revenue of over $50,000 were producing books in Canada with one-third of the publishers being primarily French language and two-thirds being English.[4] Approximately 41 percent of these firms were located in

Ontario, and they provided 74 percent of the total full-time employment; whereas 35 percent were located in Quebec providing 19 percent of the total full-time employment.[5] There were 8,126 titles published with 5,751 or 71 percent of them being in English and 2,375 or 29 percent being in French.[6]

A knowledge of the organization of the trade can be gained from the Book and Periodical Council, which is the umbrella organization for the English language book trade in Canada.[7] The Council has thirteen full-member associations representing various aspects of the trade ranging from writing, editing, publishing, manufacturing, distribution, and the selling and lending of books and periodicals. Through the Council a selector can establish contacts with the member organizations such as the Association of Canadian Publishers, the Canadian Book Publishers' Council, the Canadian Booksellers' Association, and the Canadian Magazine Publishers' Association among others.

For locating associations, individual publishers, or wholesalers, the annual *Book Trade in Canada: With Who's Where/L'Industrie du livre au Canada: Avec où trouver qui* provides the broadest coverage of the field. The directory's largest section lists "Publishers, Distributors, Sales Agents, Wholesalers and Packagers." The entries in this section contain brief informative profiles of the firms. Each entry begins with a complete address and gives the major activity of the firm, e.g., book publisher, distributor, etc. Then the publishing program is briefly described including the number of titles in print and number of titles published in the last year. A general section states when the firm was established, the number of employees, and hours of business, and the entry concludes with a list of the major officers of the firm. Other sections on literary awards, booksellers (arranged by province), and on publishing organizations and governmental organizations are also of use to the selector. Another publication, the *Canadian Publishers Directory,* issued twice a year to subscribers of *Quill & Quire,* is limited to address information but is more current for changing addresses and distribution rights especially when supplemented with the monthly updates, agency changes, and corrections appearing in *Quill & Quire.* The major sections of interest in this *Directory* are the separate English and French book sources and an audiovisual section.

Quill & Quire is the journal for the English language Canadian book trade and an exceptionally useful tool for any selector of Canadiana. Self-described as Canada's magazine of book news and reviews, the magazine describes its reading audience as "publishers, booksellers, librarians, suppliers to the trade, writers and teachers across Canada."[8] This newsprint monthly has four regular sections: News, Reviews, Books for Young People, and Bookends (the classifieds); plus, each issue has a feature topic. The feature topics include the spring and fall previews and announcements, an education issue, conference issues (both booksellers and libraries), and other subjects of interest. The news section informs the selector of the current issues in the Canadian book trade covering topics such as federal publishing policy, the formation, merger and closure of firms, small presses, and the federal GST tax. Among the regular columns in this section are a digest of news, editorial columns on publishing and libraries, and a book news column. A subscription also includes the biannual *Canadian Publishers Directory* and the monthly *Forthcoming Books/Livres à paraître*, the Canadian CIP list. With the announcements, reviews, Books for Young People (all of which will be treated later in the chapter), and the wide range of news coverage, this magazine is necessary reading for anyone who wants to be informed about Canadian publishing.

Livre d'ici, the Quebec French counterpart, is issued ten times a year from September to June. It has articles on the trade and a news column. The November issue on the annual Salon du livre de Montréal, the bibliographic essays on topics such as national unity and Montreal, the awards column, the new catalogs column, and the "Nouveautés" section at the back that indexes new titles received are all of use to the selector.

Book Selection

For the book selector, currency of information is critical in many subject areas and always remains a constant concern of the alert selector. Publishers' advertisements, flyers, and catalogs require continual attention. Once the selector has identified the major publishers in the field, particular attention should be paid to the professional associations, research centers, and special societies who publish. A selector should be sure to be placed on the appropriate mailing lists.[9] In addition to such specific sources there are more general tools to be used for current acquisition.

ADVANCE NOTICE

Both the trade and the National Library of Canada provide tools that give advance notice for many Canadian publications. *Quill & Quire* publishes spring and fall previews in January and July and spring and fall announcements in their March and September issues with the previews and announcements covering the first and last six months of the year respectively. The previews are articles reviewing the highlights of the trade releases for the upcoming season. The scope of the announcements coverage is limited to English language books with an emphasis on trade titles (caveat: "books restricted to professional or specialist markets are not included").[10] Only Canadian titles are included, and their definition of Canadian states "that a book must have at least one of the following: Canadian author, illustrator, or translator; significant Canadian content; or an originating Canadian publisher."[11] The announcements are arranged alphabetically within forty-four subject categories with title and author indexes following. Each entry contains sufficient information (imprint and price) for ordering followed by a one-sentence description, month of publication, indication if currently available, and publisher's code. The code refers to entries in the *Canadian Publishers Directory* received along with a subscription to *Quill & Quire*. The announcements provide the selector with a great snapshot overview of what's coming out this season. After thoroughly reviewing those titles in your primary subject section, the remaining announcements can be browsed to pick up related titles of interest.

Although *Livre d'ici,* the Quebec counterpart of *Quill & Quire,* does not carry spring and fall announcements, each issue lists new arrivals in the "Nouveautés" column at the back. Titles are divided into the Dewey classification categories and basic imprint information, price, an ISBN number, and a brief description of the work are given.

Another tool providing pre-publication information is the National Library of Canada's *Forthcoming Books/Livres à paraître,* which lists the CIP (cataloging in publication) records. The publication "attempts to provide advance information on the books of all Canadian publishers so that it can be used by libraries and booksellers in selecting, ordering and cataloguing books."[12] This publication is distributed monthly by *Quill & Quire* and in the ten annual issues of *Livre d'ici.* Entries are arranged alphabetically under the broad Dewey classification divisions. Each entry has full CIP cataloging with the titles being cataloged in their respective languages. In 1991 the program cataloged over 6,800 titles received from over 1,400 publishers. Although not comprehensive it offers fairly extensive pre-publication coverage of Canadian publishers.[13] The subject headings, series entries, and other information that come with the cataloging when combined with the currency of the entries make this list a very valuable selection tool. However, the selector must remember that this is CIP cataloging and titles can change between CIP cataloging and publication.

A final source listing books that have been recently published is *Current Canadian Books,* produced by the vendor, John Coutts Library Services. This monthly bibliography lists English and French titles that have been processed by the Coutts approval department within the previous month. Entries are arranged alphabetically under broad LC classification groups with a section at the back for non-Canadian imprints, i.e., Canadian authors and subjects published outside Canada. Sufficient information is included in the entries for ordering. The number of titles listed varies from 250 to 400 per month. Although not intended to be comprehensive, this list turns up titles not found elsewhere and alerts the selector to the actual appearance of titles.

CURRENT

Books in Canada stands out as the best, current national review. Their editorial policy is to review books written by a Canadian or about Canada. Traditionally known for their coverage of literature, in the last two years they have made a conscious shift broadening their coverage to include political works and other culturally significant books. Their general policy is to review English language books including translations of French Canadian publications. However, in a recent issue, reviews of the French language Governor General's candidates were included. Recent theme issues have been on writing in Quebec, Atlantic Provinces writers, and one on the prairies. Major articles on native literature, small presses, book design, culturally significant books of 1991, and literary criticism have recently appeared. Regular features include an author interview, an excerpt from a work in progress, and a profile of another author. The signed reviews are serious, critical, and will assist the selector in making selection decisions. In addition to the main review section, there are "departments" for brief reviews, reviews of poetry, first novels, theater books, and children's books. While more current, the reviews in *Quill & Quire* are shorter and less critical.

Several regional reviews are also useful for current acquisitions. *Lettres québecoises: revue de l'actualité littéraire* focuses on French Quebec literature and complements the literary coverage of *Books in Canada*. Two other regional reviews, which are printed on newsprint and delivered in bulk to bookstores for free distribution, can alert the selector to local imprints that may not be reviewed in national reviews. *Atlantic Books Today* provides coverage of local imprints (both English and French Acadian imprints). *BC Bookworld* gives a similar range of information for the most western province of the nation. Accepting the popular, promotional intent of these two reviews, the selector can glean quite a bit of useful information on the regional book trade and certainly improve coverage.

The catalogs of current publications that are published jointly by groups of Canadian publishers can also provide the selector with an informative overview of the current releases. The annual *Books on Canada/Livres sur le Canada*, which is published by the Association for the Export of Canadian books in conjunction with three publishers' associations, lists over four hundred English and French language titles relating to all fields of Canadian studies.[14] The 1993 catalog provides full order information along with a brief description for each title, and for orders from abroad two Canadian suppliers are suggested. Biennial catalogs of Canadian publications on themes such as native studies and women's studies are issued by the Canadian Book Information Centre.[15] The catalogs include relevant titles from the back lists of participating publishers and have the merit of bringing together many of the publications on the topic. The Playwrights Union of Canada, which distributes most produced Canadian plays and handles performance rights, publishes the *Catalogue of Canadian Plays*.[16] A group of Canadian small press publishers called the Literary Press Group lists all titles available in the United States in the catalog of a United States distributor named In-Book.[17] Although not as frequent in appearance as the reviews and promotional in intent, these catalogs bring together under one cover most of the new and back-listed publications in a field.

SCHOLARLY REVIEWS

For the academic selector Canadian scholarly journals are published in all the major disciplines, and most of them have a review section that includes many reviews of Canadian titles and in some cases may have a policy of only reviewing Canadian titles. Although not as current as the popular reviews, these journals can serve selectors in several ways. If selecting with limited funds, waiting for the critical scholarly reviews ensures expenditures are made only on the most significant contributions to the field. When selecting with a broader scope, the reviews often bring to attention foreign imprints, specialized scholarly works, and relevant titles in other disciplines that might not have been noticed elsewhere. Some of the most useful titles are *Canadian Literature/Littérature canadienne* (the best single source for scholarly review of Canadian literature), *Canadian Historical Review,* and the *British Journal of Canadian Studies* (the most extensive book reviews section in a Canadian studies journal).[18] André Senécal's *Canada: A Reader's Guide/Introduction bibliographique* contains a list of the major, scholarly Canadian journals where titles such as *Resources for Feminist Research/Documentation sur la recherche féministe* (which treats the interdisciplinary subject of women's studies with an annual review issue and regular reviews) can be found.[19]

The area of Canadian literature also receives two annual assessments. The *University of Toronto Quarterly* fall issue entitled "Letters in Canada" contains review essays on English and French Canadian novels, poetry, drama, and theater. Selected titles from the year are reviewed in each of these areas. The *Journal of Commonwealth Literature* December issue has a bibliography of Canadian literature accompanied with an introductory essay. The essay provides an invaluable survey of developments in Canadian literature for the year. This broad overview includes comments on subjects such as the state of Canadian publishing, new reference works, native literature, children's literature, and social history as well as the more traditional topics. It provides a very useful, concise summary of the year. The bibliography aims at comprehensiveness and includes, along with the major topics, sections on bibliographies (divided into general, serial, authors, and research aides), translations, non-fiction, and journals (cessations and new titles). The two assessments serve different purposes. The critical reviews of selected titles in "Letters in Canada" can assist in narrowing down selections. In the *Journal of Commonwealth Literature* the broader focus of the essay presents a very useful snapshot of the year's developments, and the following bibliography enables the selector to identify and order any titles that might have been missed.

COMPREHENSIVE COVERAGE

A truly comprehensive list of Canadiana provides the selector with an invaluable tool that can be used in many ways. The list itself provides the selector with a sense of the universe of publications from which selections are to be made. If a selector is collecting comprehensively in a defined subject area, the list comprises a goal to be attained. For an institution that places selective, firm orders, the list provides the universe of publications available, and by using the list the selector can be assured that the best choices are being made with the limited funds available for acquisition. When working with a vendor's approval plan, the selector can use the list both for making additional selections that fall outside the profile of the approval plan and for monitoring the vendor's performance within the profiles.

In a recent, extensive revision of collection policy the National Library of Canada has strengthened its focus on the goal of comprehensively collecting current Canadiana, and the Library now maintains the most comprehensive, current acquisitions program of Canadiana. The National Library of Canada's publication *Canadiana: Canada's National Bibliography/La Bibliographie Nationale du Canada* provides the most comprehensive coverage of publications related to Canada for selectors who want to be aware of the full range of publications available. This national bibliography includes material published in Canada through legal deposit and "includes material published in other countries if the author is a Canadian citizen, a resident of Canada, or if the publication is Canadian in subject."[20] It includes monographs, serials, pamphlets, theses, atlases, microforms, kits, sheet music and scores, sound recordings, federal, provincial, and municipal documents while excluding films, filmstrips, videotapes, videodiscs, videocassettes, other non-book materials, and maps.[21]

Canadiana is currently issued in microfiche and machine-readable records on tape. (Through 1992 a print version had also been published.) It includes Canadian Cataloguing in Publication records gathered from the extensive program run by the National Library, and the overall currency of records makes this bibliography a valuable selection tool. In the fiche edition the complete entries are in two registers. Register 1 includes Canadian imprints, and Register 2 covers foreign imprints of Canadian interest or association. These registers are arranged numerically by computer-assigned numbers. Six indexes provide access to the registers. The indexes are (1) author/title/series, (2) English subject headings, (3) French subject headings, (4) ISBN, (5) ISSN, and (6) Dewey decimal classification. Each index entry includes a brief description of the publication. With the cessation of the print copy, selectors are forced to use the Dewey index for subject selection. Although awkward and time-consuming (the selector may have to go to the register to get complete information for ordering), this is currently the only way to approach comprehensive coverage for a subject.[22] The National Library is in the preliminary stages of investigating the publishing of *Canadiana* on CD-ROM. If this is realized, it could remove many of the difficulties involved in selecting from the fiche.

The monthly *Bibliographie du Québec* is the Quebec counterpart. Its coverage includes the books, pamphlets, serials, microforms, music, and maps published in Quebec and received on legal deposit by the Bibliothèque Nationale du Québec. The monthly issues are divided into monographs and serials sections with both including government and private publications. The monograph section is arranged according to the Library of Congress classification, and the serials section is arranged alphabetically. A third section on maps is added quarterly in March, June, September, and December. Full bibliographic information is provided for each entry. Author, title, and subject indexes appear in each issue and are cumulated annually.

CANADIAN BOOK REVIEW ANNUAL

For selectors who elect not to use *Canadiana,* there are several other useful works that can serve as a safety net or final check for coverage. Notable among these is *Canadian Book Review Annual,* which reviews English language trade books with a Canadian imprint. Selected federal government documents, translations, and educational titles with a trade appeal are also included. The 5,128 reviews in the 1990 issue are divided into five broad subject areas with forty-three subdivisions. The original, signed reviews, which are evaluative and run from two hundred to five hundred words, provide real assistance to the selector. Full bibliographic information is included for ordering, and each volume has a list of publishers' addresses and an index for author, title, and subject. The focus on trade publications and the sections on children's and young adult literature make this work useful to public librarians. However, being an annual it does lack currency.

CHECKLISTS

In addition to the various annual reviews, several journals regularly include bibliographical essays on new works related to either a region of Canada or a research area. Many of these overlap and checking them can rapidly realize the law of diminishing returns. However, if used judiciously, they can become the sources that enable the selector to develop a truly exceptional collection in a well-defined subject area. *Acadiensis, BC Studies, Newfoundland Studies,* and *Revue d'histoire de l'Amérique française* issue running, regional bibliographies on the Atlantic provinces, British Columbia, Newfoundland, and Quebec respectively. Journals with running bibliographies in subject areas include *Canadian Historical Review, Canadian Ethnic Studies, Histoire sociale/Social History* (a current bibliography on the history of Canadian population and historical demography in Canada), *ICCS Contact CIEC* (this newsletter for the International Council for Canadian Studies lists foreign publications and theses relating to Canadian studies), *Journal of Canadian Art History* (recent publications and theses and dissertations), and *Labour/Le Travail* (recent publications in Canadian labor history). The previous installments of these bibliographies can be very useful in retrospective collection building and collection assessment.

CORE COLLECTIONS

In a library just starting to build a Canadiana collection, the need for the retrospective acquisition of key Canadian titles often arises. Any selective bibliographies of these core titles that can be identified greatly simplify this task. One such bibliography is André Senécal's *Canada: A Reader's Guide/ Introduction bibliographique* published in 1991. This selective, bilingual, annotated bibliography of 1,500 titles "identifies important reference materials and titles in the major disciplines taught in Canadian studies or researched outside Canada".[23] Important scholarly journals, newspapers, and mass culture periodicals are also included. The compilers have been especially selective with works published before 1975 with the result that 85 percent of the titles bear a post-1980 imprint and only 12 percent of the titles are out of print at the date of publication. Among the areas excluded are biographies, children's literature, works of literary or artistic criticism devoted to a single work or author, and business materials. The language coverage is limited to works in English or French. The work is divided into a monographs section, which is further subdivided into eleven subject sections based on the Dewey classification, and a serials section. Each entry has a full bibliographic description, an indication as to whether the title is in print, and price. This work will be an invaluable tool for any librarian attempting to develop a core collection for study or research in Canadian studies. Senécal also prepared an equally useful guide for Quebec entitled *A Reader's Guide to Quebec Studies* in 1988 which has 1,200 entries.

In contrast to Senécal's scholarly focus, *Canadian Selection: Books and Periodicals for Libraries* compiled in 1985 contains titles chosen with small or medium-sized public libraries in mind. Intended as a selective guide to significant Canadian books and periodicals for adults, the annotated bibliography includes entries for more than five thousand English language books and 255 periodicals. Only titles in print as of 1983 are included. The work is divided into four parts: a classified bibliography of the books, a periodicals section, a Canadian literary awards section, and an index. The books section is arranged by the Dewey classification. Each entry has full bibliographic information, order information, and very brief, signed annotations. Recognizing that this work is more inclusive than selective (5,000 entries compared to Senécal's 1,500), and now dated, it can still be usefully used for retrospective collection building employing, for example, the lists of awards, the periodicals list, and using the annotations to make selections from the books section. Other more specialized core lists will be mentioned as the topics arise.

VENDORS AND DEALERS

The major wholesaler of Canadiana to both Canadian institutions and the rest of the world is John Coutts Library Services Ltd. Coutts supplies monographs and continuations, but not serials, to customers throughout the world. They offer either an approval plan or selection slip services for both English and French language Canadian publications in addition to their firm order services. Their *Current Canadian Books* (described above in the Advance Notice section) is of special interest as a means of alerting selectors to specialized, scholarly publications and Canadiana published outside of Canada. Another alternative is to identify a Canadian bookstore with good stock and order from them.

In Quebec there are no vendors like Coutts. However, many of the larger bookstores also supply libraries. Some of the major bookstores offering this service are: Agence du Livre, Librarie Champigny, Librairie Flammarion, Librairie Raffin, and Librairie Renaud-Bray. The Renaud-Bray bookstore offers selection slips for French language Quebec imprints that several Canadian libraries use and has just begun an approval plan service. Another firm that specializes in export but will only take firm orders is Exportlivre.[24]

AVAILABILITY

Often during the selection process the question will arise as to whether the title under consideration is still available from the publisher and at what price. If the title is found to be in print, the acquisition process is comparatively straightforward, and the price is set. If out of print, the chances of acquiring the title decrease significantly; the work involved in the process increases; and the price becomes a major unknown variable. For Canadian imprints the question of whether a book is in print can be easily resolved, in most cases, with two works: *Canadian Books in Print* and *Les Livres disponibles canadiens de langue française*.

Canadian Books in Print is issued in two parts: an *Author and Title Index* and a *Subject Index*. The *Author and Title Index* appears annually in hard copy with complete microfiche editions in April, July, and October of each year. The work is intended to cover all titles bearing the imprint of Canadian publishers or originated by Canadian subsidiaries of international publishing firms with the listings being based on information supplied by the publishers, often in advance of publication. English language books are the main focus with French language titles published by predominantly English language publishers and French language publishers outside of Quebec being included. It does not include maps, sheet music, newspapers, periodicals and catalogs, microfiche, most government documents, and annuals not considered to be of general interest. The 1993 edition, which appeared early in 1993, contained 35,805 entries including 5,025 entries with a 1992 imprint. The work is divided into three sections: an author index, a title index, and a publisher index. The latter index, which also appears in the *Subject Index,* is another useful source for identifying lesser-known publishers.

The *Subject Index,* which only appears annually in hard copy, has the same criteria for inclusion. It is divided into three sections: a list of subject headings, the subject index, and a publisher index. The subject headings are based on the Library of Congress subject headings supplemented by Canadian headings. A special feature is the inclusion of literary works and biography. This index can be especially useful for selectors starting some retrospective collection building since the entries under the desired subject list what is currently in print on the subject.

A Canadiana selector should keep in mind that the two volumes of *Canadian Books in Print* cover all Canadian imprints, whether Canadian in content or not and do not cover titles of interest published outside of Canada. Nevertheless, the work must be recognized as one of the essential bibliographic tools for building a Canadiana collection.

The Quebec equivalent *Les Livres disponibles canadiens de langue française* has cumulations that appear quarterly in hard copy and ten times a year in microfiche. The work includes French language publications in Canada. The publications of several Ontario publishers, two New Brunswick publishers, and one publisher each from Manitoba, Saskatchewan, and British Columbia are included in addition to the extensive coverage of Quebec. The paper edition appears in three volumes: author, title, and subject, with the subject volume employing the Dewey classification for a subject breakdown. Each volume also has a list of suppliers. Like *CBIP,* this is a basic collection building tool.

REFERENCE

For either the selector just beginning to build Canadiana holdings or the librarian maintaining an extensive, research collection, well-chosen reference works constitute an essential part of their collection building strategy. Many reference tools also serve as current selection aids and are invaluable in retrospective collection building and collection assessment.

For current selection two sources provide pre-publication information for reference tools. The *Quill & Quire* spring and fall announcements, which cover most Canadian publishers, have a reference section. The monthly *Forthcoming Books/Livres à paraître,* published by the National Library and distributed by *Quill & Quire* and *Livre d'ici,* provides the selector with CIP cataloging of reference works from publishers participating in the program. Arranged by Dewey classification, the 000 generalities section lists most of the reference tools. For post-publication coverage *Canadiana* should be used for comprehensive coverage.

Before 1993 the *Canadian Library Journal* offered professional reviews of reference tools. The regular department "Reference Reviews: Selected reviews of recent Canadian reference works" offered full reviews of three to five works in each of the bimonthly issues. Annually in the February issue a checklist of reference titles that appeared in the previous year was published under the department "Reference Titles 1991." The list covered English, French, and other language titles (Inuit for example), and provided the selector with an annual safety-net checklist to make sure that no reference titles were overlooked. With the suspension of *Canadian Library*

Journal in 1993, these reviews will appear in *Feliciter,* the newsletter of the Association. More scholarly reviews of mainly bibliographical works appear in the semiannual *Papers of the Bibliographical Society of Canada/ Cahiers de la Société bibliographique du Canada.* With reviews in both English and French, about three-quarters of the twenty to twenty-five reviews in each issue are of Canadian works. *American Reference Book Annual* also offers a substantial coverage of English language, Canadian reference publications. A final check for English language titles, if desired, can be made in the *Canadian Book Review Annual.*

With reference works frequently playing an important role in the process of selection, it is essential for the selector to be aware of all the reference tools in the field. The most useful work is *Canadian Reference Sources: A Selective Guide* compiled by Dorothy Ryder and published in 1981 by the Canadian Library Association.[25] With about four thousand annotated entries of English and French titles grouped in the broad subject areas of general reference works, history, humanities, sciences, and social sciences, this work offers the best retrospective coverage of the area through 1980. A new, bilingual edition being prepared by the National Library of Canada will more than double the number of entries with increased coverage both in subject range and depth of coverage.[26] In the interim the *Guide to Reference Materials for Canadian Libraries,* 1992, 8th ed., edited by Kirsti Nilsen, lists many new electronic sources and offers updated information on the established works. Although intended primarily as a guide for library school students and covering far more than Canadian tools, this work offers up-to-date, annotated entries on new Canadian reference works covering mainly English language works. *Les Ouvrages de référence du Québec* edited by Réal Bosa and published in 1969 by the Bibliothèque Nationale du Québec provides the Quebec counterpart to Ryder. Arranged along broad subject areas, this work attempts to provide exhaustive coverage of Quebec reference works published through 1966 with an annotated list of 609 entries. An initial supplement entitled *Les Ouvrages de référence du Québec: Supplement 1967–1974* provides an additional 585 entries, and a second supplement, covering 1974–81, produces another 560 entries.

SERIALS

From the major magazines of the nineteenth century to Canadian titles that span the twentieth century such as *Saturday Night* (1887–), *Maclean's* (1911–), *Canadian Forum* (1920–), and *Chatelaine* (1928–) the challenge facing Canadian publishers has remained remarkably the same. They have to compete for a limited Canadian market against larger foreign publishers (early on British and French, now American) who have significant advantages due to economy of scale. Add to this the challenges of the market being divided into two languages and geographically stretched out along a narrow corridor with all the associated distribution problems, and it is remarkable that many magazines survived. That they grew is a testimony to their vitality and to Canadians' commitment to maintaining their distinct cultural identity. Currently a large range of titles is available for selection with titles coming from all regions and better reflecting the regional diversity of Canada.

TRADE ORGANIZATIONS

The Canadian Magazine Publishers' Association (formerly the Canadian Periodical Publishers' Association) is a national, non-profit, association representing Canadian magazines which was established in 1973. The association has over three hundred magazine members and assists them in distribution, professional development, lobbying, and promotion. Their annual subscription catalog entitled *Canadian Magazines for Everyone* is described below.

CURRENT SELECTION

Canadiana offers one approach to the challenge of keeping track of new serial titles that should be considered.[27] Although cumbersome for this purpose, the coverage is complete. Other approaches include relying upon advertisements, sample issues, and reviews, and checking the Canadian serials indexes for any new titles added.

Once established, many Canadian serials appear in the major U.S. vendors' catalogs and in the major U.S. serials tools (*Ulrich's* online lists 8,362 titles with the publisher's address in Canada). The *Canadian Serials Directory* provides the most useful information for the selection of Canadian serials and the best coverage of any work devoted to the topic. English, French, and other language publications are included in the alphabetical list of titles. The entries vary in completeness but always have the basic information such as address and price and may include information on the history, indexing, circulation, and advertising policy of the serial. Separate subject and publisher indexes appear at the back. The greatest drawback is the infrequency of publication; it has appeared in 1972, 1976, and 1987. However, a new edition is being planned. In the meantime, the *Canadian Almanac & Directory* or the *Corpus Almanac & Canadian Sourcebook* can be used for current addresses.

For the selector seeking a minimal core list of Canadian titles suitable for a public library or an academic library that does not place a major emphasis on Canadiana, other useful sources may be used. A *Library*

Journal article entitled "Northern Exposure" selects thirteen basic Canadian magazines.[28] Although limited to English language publications, the titles cover a broad range of subjects and each title is described in terms of its scope and special features. All thirteen are indexed in *Canadian Periodical Index* and *Canadian Index* with seven being indexed in *Magazine Index* and *Magazine Index Plus* and one in *Reader's Guide*. Prices (now slightly out of date) and order information for all the titles are provided at the end of the article. A slightly broader coverage of thirty-five titles appears in the "Canada" section of the sixth edition (1989) of *Magazines for Libraries*. This list includes French and English publications and has more complete information on the titles such as intended audience and full information on where the title is indexed. Accepting the stated tendency to emphasize the social sciences and history, this list has the most useful information and a well-balanced coverage. For a broader range of selection the Canadian Magazine Publishers' Association produces an annual catalog entitled *Canadian Magazines for Everyone*. The 1992 catalog lists over 245 titles divided into ten broad subject areas. The catalog is free to libraries and is available from the Association.[29] The best core list of scholarly journals will be found in Senécal's *Canada: A Reader's Guide/Introduction bibliographique*.

VENDORS

Faxon Canada Ltd. and Canebsco Subscription Services Ltd. are two Canadian firms that have affiliations with major international vendors. Both companies have an expertise in supplying Canadian titles. A comparison of service charges should help decide which vendor to select. Canebsco can supply a catalog of Canadian titles. One Quebec vendor is Periodica.

INDEXING

A good periodical index forms the cornerstone of a Canadian periodicals collection. Two indexes are available: the *Canadian Periodical Index (CPI)* published by Info Globe and the new *Canadian Index (CI)* published by Micromedia, each with their own strengths.[30] Both are available online and in CD-ROM. The hard copy for both appears monthly with semiannual cumulations for *CI* and annual for *CPI*. *CI* has broader coverage, indexing approximately six hundred titles (including eight daily newspapers) compared to approximately four hundred titles for *CPI*. *CI*'s strengths of coverage lie in the newspapers indexed, a very strong coverage of business and trade journals, popular magazines, and more academic titles in the social sciences and medicine. *CPI* is bilingual and indexes more Quebec French language journals than *CI*. Articles in *CPI* are listed under English subject headings with cross-references from the equivalent French headings. The coverage of *CPI* is better in the area of literary small press journals and it includes three Canadian studies journals published outside of Canada. Retrospective coverage for *CPI* begins in 1920 whereas *CMI*, the predecessor of *CI*, commences in 1985. If one is willing to sacrifice some currency for CD-ROM access, the *Canadian Business and Current Affairs* CD-ROM (the CD-ROM equivalent of *CI* often referred to as *CBCA*) again offers significantly broader coverage than the *CPI* CD-ROM. If more extensive Quebec French language coverage is required, *Point de repère: Index analytique d'articles de périodiques de langue française*, published by the Bibliothèque Nationale du Québec in Quebec City, should be acquired. Also available online as *REPERE*, the hard copy appears ten times a year with annual cumulations. Two hundred and seventy-five French language periodicals are indexed with the majority of them coming from Quebec, seventy from Europe, and twelve from the rest of Canada.

News

NEWSPAPERS

The national edition of the *Globe & Mail* (published in Toronto) is generally regarded as Canada's national paper. The Quebec French language counterpart is *Le Devoir*, published in Montreal. For greater regional coverage the following newspapers could be added: the *Halifax Chronicle Herald*, *Montreal Gazette* (English language), *Toronto Star*, *Winnipeg Free Press*, and the *Vancouver Sun*. The *Gale Directory of Publications* (formerly *Ayer Directory of Publications*) will provide the necessary order information.

INDEXES

The hard copy *Canadian Index* and the CD-ROM *CBCA*, published by Micromedia in Toronto, provide selected indexing to the eight English language daily newspapers (the six listed above, the *Calgary Herald*, and the *Financial Post*). The Quebec counterpart is *L'Index de l'Actualité*, published by Inform II (Microfor in Montreal). It selectively indexes four French language newspapers: *Le Devoir*, *La Presse*, *Le Soleil*, and *Le Journal de Montréal*.

NEWS MAGAZINES

Two news magazines complement the daily newspapers. *Maclean's: Canada's Weekly Magazine* is the English Canadian news magazine. With full-text reference online on Info Globe, Infomart Online, and NEXIS and indexing in the *Magazine Index* and three Canadian indexes, it is essential reading for current Canadian affairs. *L'Actualité,* which appears twenty times per year, is French Canada's leading current affairs periodical. These two titles are basic for any coverage of current Canadian events.

Government Publications

The selector of Canadian government publications encounters many of the challenges met in the selection of publications from most of the countries of the world. Bibliographical control is not complete, publicity is often lacking, and identifying the retail outlet where the publication can be purchased takes some effort. However, Canadian government publications offer an invaluable resource of information about the country essential for any Canadiana collection, and several, useful selection tools exist. A knowledge of the structure of government in Canada greatly assists the selector, and an introduction to this subject can be acquired from Brian Land's up-do-date chapter "Government Publications: A Description and Guide to the Use of Canadian Government Publications" in *Politics: Canada* (1991) and Olga Bishop's more extensive *Canadian Official Publications* (1981).[31]

CURRENT SELECTION

The *Weekly Checklist of Canadian Government Publications/Liste hebdomadaire des publications du gouvernement du Canada,* also known as the "pink list," offers the most current coverage of federal government publications. Designed for use by both depository and non-depository libraries, this bilingual list covers items sent to full depository libraries, providing both the Canadian and the foreign price (in U.S. dollars) and the catalog number for ordering.[32] Complementing this is the *Special List of Canadian Government Publications/Liste speciale des publications du gouvernement du Canada.* This bilingual publication lists free and priced publications that are not sent to depository libraries. Known as the "green list," it appears monthly. The *Government of Canada Publications/Publications du gouvernement du Canada: Quarterly Catalogue trimestriel* contains all publications included in the *Weekly Checklists* and *Special Lists* along with an appendix listing periodicals and other subscription services. Some departments and agencies such as Statistics Canada issue their own catalogs or checklists.

The *Statistics Canada Catalogue 1990* merits further consideration because of both the high interest in the subject and the good organization of the catalog that makes it easy to use.[33] Published in both English and French the catalog has indexing by author, title, and subject and includes sections on mapping services and microdata files. In addition a series of useful appendixes cover such topics as how to order, how to get more help, and data available in other formats (electronic mainframe data, CD-ROM products, and microform).

The acquisition of provincial government publications is more problematic with little centralized distribution (one often has to go to the issuing department) and few periodic checklists. Brian Land's essay includes a list of "retrospective bibliographies and current checklists and catalogues of provincial and territorial government publications" that will direct the dedicated selector to the appropriate tools.[34] An article on the acquisition tools for Quebec government publications by Louise Carpentier provides a thorough review for that province.[35] An alternate solution to ordering from each province would be to use the *Microlog* index (discussed in the following "Indexes" section) to identify provincial publications and then to order microfiche copies from Micromedia.

For those selectors who do not require such in-depth coverage, *Canadiana* may provide a workable solution. Although cumbersome and not as complete as the *Quarterly Catalogue,* it provides full cataloging entries for the federal and provincial publications listed. A highly selective and somewhat dated solution can be found in the Canada section of the annual "Notable Documents" issue of *Government Publications Review.*[36] Selected on the basis of their reference value and subject coverage, 110 federal and provincial publications (with 107 of them having a 1991 or 1992 date of publication) are included in the 1992 issue. Each entry has a descriptive annotation and full order information.

Where and How . . . to Obtain Canadian Government Publications/Où et comment . . . obtenir les publications du gouvernement du Canada, published by Canada Communication Group, offers useful advice on the acquisition of Canadian federal publications.[37] The pamphlet lists Canadian bookstores that serve as outlets for government publications, major federal government departments that distribute free and priced publications, and ordering information for customers in the United States and customers from all other countries. Many government publications appear in microform and cost considerably less in that format. An annual survey of federal government publications in microform that has appeared in the last four years of *Microform Review* will enable the selector to choose titles appropriate for this format.[38]

INDEXES

Three indexes provide useful access to Canadian documents. *Canadiana* provides the same indexing for documents as it does for all other Canadian imprints cataloged. A cumulated annual index comes with the subscription to *Government of Canada Publications/Publications du gouvernement du Canada: Quarterly Catalogue trimestriel.* It provides access to the *Quarterly Catalogues* which are not cumulated. The single, most useful index for its currency and breadth of coverage is *Microlog: Canadian Research Index/Index de Recherche du Canada,* produced by Micromedia Limited. This monthly indexing service with annual cumulations offers indexing by author, series, and subject for English and French publications in the language of publication. Bilingual publications are indexed in both languages. Abstracts of each document are also provided, and the coverage includes an extensive selection of federal, provincial, and municipal documents. The *Microlog* file from 1979 is available online to Canadians only through Can/OLE, and on CD-ROM from Micromedia. The firm also serves as a major supplier of Canadian government publications, and most titles included in the index are available either in paper or in microfiche from Micromedia.

Children and Young Adults

ORGANIZATION

Founded in 1976, the Canadian Children's Book Centre constitutes a major resource for information concerning English children's literature in Canada.[39] The Centre's goal is to promote Canadian children's literature through the encouragement of reading, writing, and illustrating Canadian children's books. In addition to publications the Toronto-based Centre has a reference library, offers services to authors and illustrators, and organizes Canadian Children's Book Week. For a selector who is either interested in gaining familiarity with the field or is seeking more advanced research information, the Centre would be an ideal place to start. The Quebec counterpart is Communication—jeunesse.[40] Its goal is the promotion of Quebec literature in French for the young, and it publishes an annual bibliography and selections lists.

CURRENT SELECTION

With award-winning publishers like Tundra Books and interesting authors such as Jean Little, it is important for librarians to be aware of material for youth appearing in Canada. *CM: A Reviewing Journal of Canadian Materials for Young People* provides the best current coverage for the interested selector. Published by the Canadian Library Association six times yearly in January, March, May, September, October, and November, *CM* or *Canadian Materials* has a broad scope. Its policy is "to review all obtainable materials, in all media formats, published or produced in Canada for children and young people".[41] Even though French materials are not covered inclusively and provincial government documents are specifically excluded, this review journal provides the most extensive coverage available.[42]

Intended to assist public and school librarians in selection of materials, *CM* has sections entitled "Features," "Book Reviews," and "Video Reviews." The "Features" section includes author and illustrator profiles and, more importantly, bibliographic essays on topics such as stereotyping, French (language) immersion, and a bibliography of films and videos on the environment, all of which assist in collection building. The "Book Reviews" section divides the reviews into four groups: "Professional," "K to Grade 6" (ages 3 to 11), "Grades 7 to 9" (ages 12 to 14), and "Grades 10 and up" (ages 15 and up). Within each age grouping the books are divided into broad subject categories such as fiction, history, and nature/the environment. Reviewers are selected from teachers, school, and public librarians. The signed reviews are limited to two hundred words, include an age designation, and conclude with an evaluation that in one issue range from "highly recommended" to "cannot recommend." Although not broken up by age groups, the "Video Reviews" section has an age level assigned to each title and has the same subject divisions. Sufficient order information is provided for all works reviewed. The last pages list books received and paperback reprints with citations to the reviews of the latter group.

Several other serials can also assist in selecting current material. *Lurelu: la seule revue exclusivement consacrée à la littérature québecoise pour la jeunesse* reviews Quebec French literature for the young. Published triannually, this journal contains signed reviews with suggested age levels and recommendations. Each issue also has well-researched articles with good bibliographies, interviews, profiles, news, and prize lists.[43] Another new serial is *The Teaching Librarian,* which is the magazine of the Ontario School Library Association. It has special pull-out sections on curriculum units in every issue. Each of these units (one was on women's studies) sets out the educational goals and provides an up-to-date, selected bibliography on the topic for the working school librarian. The large "Reviews" section groups the reviews by age (primary/junior books, intermediate books, and senior books) with additional format groups of video, audio, and government publications. A short review is provided for each title along with full bibliographic description and reading levels. Each review concludes with useful suggestions as to how the title could be linked to the curriculum. Issues have articles on publishing, authors, and articles of interest to teaching librarians. The "BFYP Books for Young People" section in *Quill & Quire* offers the most current reviews but contains far fewer reviews than *CM*. Other columns offer topical essays and news relating to Canadian children's literature. *Children's Book News*, published by the Canadian Children's Book Center, has a "New Book" section at the back that lists books received with a reading and interest level for each title along with order information. Each issue also contains several pages of reviews. The Canadian-based *Emergency Librarian*, which focuses on school librarianship, often includes Canadian titles in its reviews.[44]

Several lists of selected titles exist and can be of real assistance for selective purchases or recent retrospective collection building. *Our Choice*, issued annually by the Canadian Children's Book Centre, offers an independent committee's selection of the best children's books from the previous year. The current catalog, which contains over three hundred entries with full order information and reading levels, includes the selections from the two previous years with the new additions listed separately from the back list. The irregular *Notable Canadian Children's Books/Un Choix de livres canadiens pour la jeunesse*, published by the National Library of Canada, offers a more selective choice while being less current. In 1990 *Booklist* published two selective bibliographies of English and French Canadian books for children covering the years 1987–89 and 1984–89 respectively.[45]

RETROSPECTIVE SELECTION

Sheila Egoff's and Judith Saltman's *The New Republic of Childhood: A Critical Guide to Canadian Children's Literature in English* provides a useful thematic and critical overview of the field. The bibliographies at the back of the book offer an excellent collection evaluation and retrospective building tool. For the selector starting to build a collection, the core list of almost two hundred titles in *Too Good to Miss: Classic Canadian Children's Books* can be very useful. The more extensive, bilingual *Canadian Books for Young People/Livres canadiens pour la jeunesse* last published in 1988 provides an annotated list of English and French titles then in print with suggested reading levels.[46] Magazines for young people, publisher's series, and award books are also included. The 1986 *Canadian Picture Books/Livres d'images canadiens* offers an annotated list (English for English titles and French for French) of picture books indicating "superior" titles and accompanied with a thorough subject index. The scholarly journal in the field is *Canadian Children's Literature/Littérature canadienne pour la jeunesse,* which is published by the Canadian Children's Press and Canadian Children's Literature Association. This journal has good reviews and, more importantly, regularly has bibliographic essays that can be very useful for retrospective collection building. Two recent bibliographic essays were Elspeth Ross's on "Children's Books on Contemporary North American Indian/Native/ Metis Life: A Selected Bibliography of Books and Professional Reading," and Joan Weller's "Canadian English Language Juvenile Periodicals: An Historical Overview 1847–1990."[47]

Special Formats

COMPUTER FILES

In this rapidly expanding field where traditional print terms such as "publishing" take on whole new meanings and growth seems to be outstripping any bibliographical control, a multiplicity of approaches and persistent "bibliographic" and "electronic" searching must be undertaken in order to gain any real sense of the amount of Canadian information available. The following suggestions are intended as leads to introduce the interested selector into new fields of information resources to be explored, assessed, and exploited as selection tools.

For existing computer files several directories can be consulted to locate Canadian content. A check in the subject index of the *Gale Directory of Databases: Volume 1: Online Databases* under Canada, Canadian History, and Canadiana yields 275 entries.[48] A similar check of volume two produces forty-five entries.[49] The 1992 *ESPIAL Canadian Database Directory,* available in both English and French, provides better access to Canadian information. The *Directory* contains 505 entries divided into subdivisions under the broad topics of general, social sciences, physical and applied science, and technology. In addition to the main directory there is a separate list of the 118 portable databases listed in that directory. Title, subject, producer, online services, and vendor indexes are present along with the addresses of the principal vendors. Intended as a guide to Canadian content in national and international databases, the *Directory* ranks each entry for the amount of Canadian content using four categories: 80 percent plus, 30 percent–79 percent, 5 percent–29 percent, and less than 5 percent. (Seventy-four entries fall into the less than 5 percent category.) Approximately 25 percent of the entries are in French or have French language materials. A monthly updated online version is available in French or English from SDM Inc.[50] In addition to these directories some articles have been written reviewing Canadian content in CD-ROMs.[51]

The most reliable method of maintaining current awareness of new, commercially available computer file products with Canadian content is through maintaining a close liaison with Canadian producers and vendors. A regular scanning of *Database Canada* and reviewing the diskware reviews and news columns in *Canadian CD-ROM News* will also turn up information on new products. With the government being a major producer of computer files the *Weekly Checklist* must also be scanned for new files and the *Statistics Canada Catalogue* provides the selector with an initial introduction to some of the computer files available from this department.[52] Older government computer files can be found in the National Archives of Canada.

The major commercial sources of Canadian computer files of general interest are CAN/OLE, Micromedia, Infomart, Info Globe, and SDM. CAN/OLE Canadian Online Enquiry Service is an automated information storage and retrieval system operated and maintained by the Canada Institute for Scientific and Technical Information (CISTI).[53] With its scientific focus, most of the databases available through CAN/OLE contain mainly international scientific information rather than focusing solely on Canadian content. There are, however, scientific and technical databases with a high Canadian content in areas such as water resources, agriculture, sports, standards, transportation, and the North. CAN/OLE also has *Microlog, Statistics Canada Catalogue Online, Directory of Associations in Canada,* and the National Library's Canadiana catalog, all of which offer extensive Canadian coverage outside the sciences. CAN/OLE is accessible only to Canadians. Micromedia indexes over six hundred Canadian periodicals and ten newspapers for the *Canadian Business and Current Affairs (CBCA)* database. Available in CD-ROM and online from Dialog, *CBCA* is a key bibliographic database which since 1991 has been enhanced with abstracts. Micromedia also produces other CD-ROM products (*CD: Education, Microlog,* and *Directory of Associations in Canada*) and serves as a vendor for other publishers of Canadian databases. Infomart offers eleven full-text Canadian newspapers online along with news services and financial newspapers.[54] Info Globe has offered the full text of the *Globe & Mail* online since 1979 and now on CD-ROM. It also offers the bibliographic databases *Canadian Periodical Index* both online and in CD-ROM, and *Canadian Books in Print, Canadian Who's Who,* and some Micromedia products online. SDM Services Documentaires Multimedia is the largest North American producer and vendor of French language databases.[55] Two SDM databases of particular interest are *Point de repère,* an index of 280 French language periodicals which are mainly Quebec titles, and *HISCABEQ,* the online version of *Bibliographie de l'histoire du Québec et du Canada,* which has over eighty thousand citations covering 1946 to the present. In addition to these general resources the above firms and other Canadian firms offer other more specialized online resources, especially in the area of business. For further information, Jacqueline Halupka in "Online in Canada" provides an overview of Canadian online databases, and between Susan Merry and all in "The Canadian Connection: Business Online" and Ulla De Stricker and Jane Dysart in *Business Online,* a thorough review of Canadian online business resources may be obtained.[56]

Another array of computer files exists outside the commercial marketplace in the research institutions of Canada. Although not all Canadian in content, many may contain much material of interest to the selector of Canadiana. Records describing many of these data file collections can be accessed through CULDAT (Canadian Union List of Machine Readable Data Files) at the University of Alberta. The database contains about 1,500 records from nine data libraries/archives and is searchable through electronic mail via Remote SPIRES. For further information and instructions on searching the database, the Data Librarian at the University of Alberta (E-mail address: abombak@vm.ucs.ualberta.ca) should be contacted.[57] The *Directory of Canadian University Data Libraries/Archives* contains four additional data libraries/archives who have not yet reported their holdings to CULDAT.[58] These libraries would have to be contacted directly to gather information concerning their holdings. Equally important, United States sources are the ICPSR and the Roper Center. The Center has recently published the *Roper Center Guide to Canadian Public Opinion Resources,* which summarizes the Gallup Canada collection at the Center and provides a directory of survey sources in Canada.[59]

MAPS

The bibliographical control for selection and acquisitions of the current mapping of Canada is, at best, far from adequate. No unified listing of new maps exists, leaving it up to the selector to identify the major publishers and their means of listing their new maps. As in many countries it is the agencies of the federal, provincial, and other levels of government who publish most Canadian maps, and the information they provide concerning their publications varies significantly from agency to agency. For a concise and very informative overview of modern Canadian map making and the roles played by the various government agencies, the selector should turn to the "Canada" chapter of *World Mapping Today.*[60]

The current status and availability of all federal topographical map series can be found in three index maps available upon request from the Canada Map Office.[61] The three index maps for eastern, western, and northern Canada each contain instructions on how to order maps from the Canada Map Office and information on other (general, statistics, national atlas, national parks, gazetteers, and special purpose) federal map publications. For addresses and information on a range of topics such as geological mapping (federal and provincial), federal thematic programs, the mapping activities of the provinces, and commercial map publishers, selectors should start their search with the sources provided in *World Mapping Today*. Although their material is slightly dated, with the information having been gathered in 1984–86, the authors' focus on identifying current, available maps makes it a very useful tool for the acquisition of maps.

MICROFORMS

Microforms constitute a critical segment of most long-term, retrospective, collection building plans. When faced with limited acquisition funds and space constraints, the selector can turn to microform products to help resolve these limitations while at the same time acquiring titles that seldom if ever appear on the out-of-print market. The challenge of brittle book preservation offers another pressing array of reasons for the inclusion of microforms in any plans.

In most cases selection of a microform product involves a sizable expenditure. The selector needs to have the publisher's catalog and then discuss the product with the publisher before finalizing any selection decisions. Locating the publishers, especially non-Canadian publishers, presents somewhat of a challenge. A list of publishers by country in the "Geographic Index" *Microform Marketplace: MMP; An International Directory of Micropublishing* identifies thirty-two Canadian publishers.[62] Many non-Canadian publishers with Canadian content products can be located in Suzanne Dodson's *Microform Research Collections* through the subject index.[63] Dodson also provides a thorough description and critical assessments of the research sets.

The major publishers within Canada are several commercial publishers, governmental departments, and the unique Canadian Institute of Historical Microreproductions, which offers a nearly comprehensive collection of pre-1900 Canadian monographs and serials. One of the largest commercial microform publishers is Micromedia. Based in Toronto, the company offers over seven hundred Canadian serial titles as well as government publications from the federal, provincial, and municipal levels in both their Microlog collection and other sets. McLaren Micropublishing, a smaller Toronto firm, specializes in the alternative press, social history, feminist material, and the visual arts. Two firms that specialize in newspapers are Commonwealth Microfilm Library, which offers an extensive range of historical, Canadian newspapers, and Preston Microfilming Service Ltd. The National Library of Canada's Canadian Theses Service maintains control of microform copies of over eighty thousand theses that it has microfilmed since 1965 and publishes lists and subject guides to foreign and Canadian theses about Canada and Canadians.[64] Copies of these theses are available from Micromedia Limited and UMI.[65] In Quebec the Bibliothèque Nationale du Québec has issued a series of catalogs beginning in 1975, and the Société canadienne du microfilm inc. is a Quebec commercial firm.

The Canadian Institute for Historical Microreproductions (CIHM) was established in 1978 with the goal of the collection, preservation, and distribution of printed Canadiana. Since then it has produced the largest microfiche library of pre-1900 Canadian monographs consisting of over 56,800 titles. It is now filming all pre-1900 serial titles not previously filmed. All titles included in the collections are fully cataloged, and CAN/MARC tapes of the catalog records are available with the purchase of the set. Once the pre-1900 serials are complete, CIHM will commence filming post-1900 monographs. This impressive collection forms the most extensive retrospective Canadian research collection available.

MUSIC

The best source for selecting works about music, printed music, and recorded music relating to Canada is *Canadiana*. It has covered printed music since its inception in 1950 and sound recordings since they became subject to legal deposit in September, 1969. A work is included if "there is any Canadian connection such as composer, arranger, lyricist, performer or subject even for just one work in a collection."[66] Publishers of music scores have been participating in the CIP program since 1984, but sound recordings are not yet part of the program. No other source or sources offer the selector this breadth of coverage in all the necessary formats.

For the selector who needs to know more about Canadian music the second edition of the *Encyclopedia of Music in Canada,* edited by Helmut Kallmann and Gilles Potvin and published by the University of Toronto Press in 1992, offers an informative introduction to the nation's musical culture. Addressed to a wide range of readers, the *Encyclopedia* contains over 3,100 entries and is available in English or French.

Music Directory Canada provides an overview of the trade and is published biennially by CM Books of Toronto. Although the majority of the sixty-five sections deal with aspects of the popular trade, sections such as associations, music publishers, and record distributors will be of interest.

The Canadian Music Centre in Toronto contains the national collection of music scores by the major concert composers.[67] Organized to support the work of the approximately three hundred composers who are Associates of the CMC, the Centre promotes the Associates' music by collecting, recording, reproducing, and distributing it. Copies of scores can be borrowed from the Centre. Unpublished scores can be purchased from the Centre, and the Centre can direct you to the correct publisher for the purchase of published scores. New acquisitions to their collection of over eleven thousand scores are listed in their annual publication *Acquisitions*. The Centre also distributes recorded Canadian music including their own recording label Centrediscs. A catalog of recorded music is available upon request, and the Centre will assist the selector in locating the publisher of recordings not listed in their catalog.

AUDIOVISUAL

This section focuses on film and video with a brief consideration of educational media.[68] In these areas the bibliographical control for selection varies by format. National bibliographies provide good coverage of film, video, and sound recordings with the remaining broad area of educational media needing better control.

For film and video *Film/Video Canadiana* is a national, bilingual database covering films and videos produced in Canada, co-productions with foreign companies, short films, and TV productions released for general distribution. This database is produced by the National Film Board of Canada in collaboration with the National Library of Canada, the National Archives of Canada, and Cinematheque quebecoise. The database "includes descriptive information on more than 23,000 Canadian films and videos and is growing at the rate of 2,000 titles per year."[69] Each entry has the following information: title; year of production; running time; format; one of: director, producer, or executive producer; one of: production company, distribution company, or sponsor; and a synopsis. The database also has a Directory of Producers and Distributors with addresses, telephone and fax numbers for six thousand Canadian sources. *Film/Video Canadiana* is available in CD-ROM.[70] This database provides the selector with an extensive listing of French and English films and videos produced in Canada. The National Film Board also produced a print filmography covering the same material and having the same title, *Film/Video Canadiana*. The latest edition covered the years 1987–88.[71]

For sound recordings the National Library of Canada has included bibliographic descriptions in *Canadiana* since 1969. In the case of sound recordings, the work must have Canadian content before it is listed, i.e., any Canadian connection such as composer, writer, arranger, lyricist, performer, or subject. Conversely sound recordings made in Canada without any Canadian content are not listed.

The internationally famous National Film Board of Canada constitutes the best source for both documentary and other types of films (English and French) about Canada. Founded in 1939, the NFB has the mandate to produce and distribute and to promote the production and distribution of films designed to interpret Canada to Canadians and to other nations.[72] Separate print catalogs of NFB films currently available for distribution in Canada, the United States, and internationally are available from the NFB.[73] The over 500-page catalog for Canada provides order information and a brief summary for each title listed along with general instructions on how to order it. The Board also operates film and video libraries across Canada and offices in New York, Paris, and London for the commercial distribution and sales of NFB films and videos.[74] In addition the Canadian Film Distribution Center at the State University of New York at Plattsburgh rents and sells over one thousand NFB films to educational and cultural institutions in the United States.[75] A free catalog is available from the Center.

The Canadian Filmmakers Distribution Centre, which was founded in 1967, promotes the work of independent filmmakers across Canada. In its complimentary catalogs the Centre lists over 1,200 titles of which 85 percent are Canadian.[76] These titles are distributed nationally and internationally.

In addition to government and feature films there are a large number of independent film producers in Canada. A source for identifying non-theatrical producers is Liz Avison's *Distribution Guide for Non-Theatrical 16mm Film and Video in Canada*.[77]

Many Canadian television broadcasting companies also sell videos of programs for education and institutional use, i.e., non-broadcast use. Three of these are CBC, CTV, and TVO. The Canadian Broadcasting Corporation (CBC) is an independent crown corporation with the mandate to provide comprehensive radio and TV services to English- and French-speaking Canadians. CTV is a private television company, and TVO (Television Ontario) is the educational broadcasting authority for the province of Ontario. Catalogs of programs for sale are available from all three.[78] Although not as extensive as the NFB's, these catalogs offer videos on a wide variety of contemporary Canadian topics.

Copies of earlier Canadian audiovisual material that are no longer commercially distributed can sometimes be obtained from the Audio-Visual and Cartographic Archives division of the National Archives of Canada. The Archives is the designated archives for both the CBC and the NFB. Two important guides to the collections are the *Guide to CBC Sources at the Public Archives* and the *Canadian Feature Film Index 1913–1985*.[79]

The bibliographic control of other English language audiovisual media is very incomplete. NFB multimedia products for the classroom are listed in catalogs available at the NFB's English language and French language distributors.[80] *Visual Media/Médias visuels* has English and French reviews of audiovisual material in the two languages respectively. In addition the periodical usually includes two mediographies per issue with sections on both English and French language material. Both *CM* and *Emergency Librarian* also review some videos.

The situation for French language audiovisual media is better. The database DAVID, Documents Audio VIsuels Disponibles, available online, in CD-ROM, in microfiche, and in print under the title *Choix: documentation audiovisuelle*, provides current information on new French language audiovisual materials.[81] The database includes both Canadian and foreign audiovisual publications. DAVID contains over 42,000 titles and *Choix* lists around 2,500 titles per year. SDM, the publisher of these titles, has also published two series of guides to audiovisual media, one series for children ages twelve and under, and one for young adults and adults.[82]

Antiquarian and Out-of-Print Sources

The acquisition of important out-of-print (OP) titles often makes the difference between a respectable collection and an outstanding research collection. However, the process of acquiring these titles can be prohibitively expensive if the procedures are not well thought out and monitored. Out-of-print acquisitions are labor intensive and prices of titles can vary significantly from dealer to dealer. A practical approach to this acquisition problem involves the preparation and use of desiderata lists. Recognizing the costs involved, the selector should critically scrutinize every title before adding it to the list and annually review all titles remaining on the list. Once prepared, the list may be sent to *AB Bookman*, which is widely read by Canadian OP booksellers, or the list may be sent to a dealer with instructions to search for the titles for six months or a year. If the list is sent to several booksellers at once, clear instructions to "quote from stock only" should be added.

When deciding to search for an out-of-print book the question often arises as to what is a reasonable price for the sought-after title. Several approaches can be used in the task of establishing the current price range. The standard reference tools, the *Bookman's Price Index* and the two auction records *American Book-Prices Current* and *British-Auction Records,* can be checked. If the title cannot be located in these works, a check with a known Canadiana bookseller will often establish a price range and may also locate a copy. Another alternative involves keeping files of Canadiana out-of-print catalogs and checking them.

Locating booksellers who specialize in the various fields of Canadiana can be accomplished fairly easily. Within Canada the trade organization, the Antiquarian Booksellers' Association of Canada/Association de la Librairie Ancienne du Canada, has French and English members from all across Canada. All members are experienced booksellers who can also do appraisals of collections. The Association publishes a *Membership Directory,* which lists the specialities of all members along with their addresses and phone numbers.[83] The antiquarian book trade within Canada is well developed. Although few booksellers specialize solely in Canadiana, most of them carry Canadian stock and have a field of Canadiana as one of their specialties. They often have regional strengths and many of them issue catalogs that should be acquired.

Conclusion

The rich diversity of Canada with its two official languages and varied regions can be seen in the preceding sections. Within the country an active, sophisticated publishing community mirrors the diversity of the nation by publishing a wealth of material in many formats and on a wide variety of topics. An equally wide range of selection tools exists to enable selectors to develop a Canadiana collection. These tools along with other works are mentioned to suggest new approaches to collecting Canadiana. While developing and refining the selection process selectors will, at the same time, expand and refine their knowledge of Canada and Canadiana. As the country grows and evolves, this knowledge will enable selectors to continually maintain a current collection, a collection that responds to the specific community served and anticipates future community needs. The selection of Canadiana is a dynamic learning process that fosters the growth of the community, the collection, and selectors.

Appendix A. Canadian Vendors

ENGLISH AND FRENCH BOOKS
John Coutts Library Services Ltd.
  6900 Kinsmen Court
  Niagara Falls, Ontario
  L2E 7E7

FRENCH BOOKS
Agence du Livre
  1710 rue St. Denis
  Montréal, Québec
  H2X 3K6

Exportlivre Inc.
  C.P. 305
  Saint-Lambert, Québec
  J4P 3P8

Librairie Champigny
  4380 rue St. Denis
  Montréal, Québec
  H2J 2L1

Librairie Flammarion
  Place Montréal Trust
  Niveau 1
  Montréal, Québec
  H3A 3J5

Librairie Raffin Inc.
  6722 rue St. Hubert
  Montréal, Québec
  H2S 2M6

Librairie Renaud-Bray
  5219 chemin de la Côtes-des-Neiges
  Montréal, Québec
  H3T 1Y1

FRENCH PERIODICALS

Periodica
  1155 ave. Ducharme
  Outremont, Québec
  H2V 1E2

Appendix B. Micro Publishers

COMMERCIAL: GOVERNMENT
PUBLICATIONS, REPORTS, SERIALS

Micromedia
  20 Victoria St.
  Toronto, Ontario
  M5C 2N8

COMMERCIAL: ETHNIC
NEWSPAPERS, MINORITY GROUPS

McLaren Micropublishing Ltd.
  P.O. Box 972, Station F
  Toronto, Ontario
  M4Y 2N9

COMMERCIAL: NEWSPAPERS

Commonwealth Microfilm Library
Marketing Division
  3395 American Drive, Unit 11
  Mississauga, Ontario
  L4V 1T5

Preston Microfilming Service Ltd.
  2215 Queen St. East
  Toronto, Ontario
  M4E 1E8

Société canadienne du microfilm inc./
Canadian Microfilming Company
  464 St. Jean
  Montréal, Québec
  H2Y 2S1

GOVERNMENT

Bibliothèque nationale du Québec
Service de la conservation et de la
reproduction
Microphotographie
  125 rue Sherbrooke Ouest
  Montréal, Québec
  H2X 1X4

Canadian Theses Service
National Library of Canada
  395 Wellington St.
  Ottawa, Ontario
  K1A 0N4

NON-PROFIT/PRESERVATION

Canadian Institute for Historical
Microreproductions
  P.O. Box 2428, Station D
  Ottawa, Ontario
  K1P 5W5

Appendix C. Selection Sources

BOOK TRADE

Canadian Publishers Directory. v. 1– . 1967– . Toronto: Quill & Quire. Biannual.
Thorne, Eunice, and Ed Matheson. *The Book Trade in Canada 1990/91: With Who's Where/L'Industrie du livre au Canada 1990/91: avec où trouver qui.* v. 1– . 1967– . Ottawa: Ampersand. Annual.

CURRENT SELECTION

Advance Notice

Forthcoming Books/Livres à paraître. Ottawa: National Library of Canada. v. 1– . 1976– . Ottawa: National Library of Canada. Monthly.
Livre d'ici. v. 1– . 1975– . Montréal: Livre d'ici. 10/yr.
Quill & Quire. v. 1– . 1935– . Toronto: Key Publishers. Monthly.

Current

Atlantic Books Today. v. 1– . 1992– . Halifax: Atlantic Provinces Book Review Society. Triannually.
BC Bookworld. v. 1– . 1987– . Vancouver: A.R.T. Bookworld Productions. Quarterly.
Books in Canada. v. 1– . 1971– . Toronto: Canadian Review of Books. 9/yr.
Books on Canada/Livres sur le Canada. 1980– . Ottawa: Association for the Export of Canadian Books. Annual. (Address: 504-1 Nicholas St., Ottawa, Ontario, Canada K1N 7B7.)
Catalogue of Canadian Plays. 1972?– . Toronto: Playwright Union of Canada. Irregular. (Address: Playwright Union of Canada, 54 Wolseley St., 2nd Floor, Toronto, Ontario, Canada M5T 1A5.)
Current Canadian Books. v. 1– . 1971– . Niagara Falls, Ontario: John Coutts Library Services. Monthly.
Lettres québecoises. v. 1– . 1976– . Montreal: Editions Jumonville. Quarterly.

Scholarly Reviews

British Journal of Canadian Studies. v. 1– . 1986– . Edinburgh: British Association for Canadian Studies. Biannual.
Canadian Historical Review. v. 1– . 1920– . Toronto: University of Toronto Press. Quarterly.
Canadian Literature/Littérature canadienne. v. 1– . 1959– . Vancouver: University of British Columbia Press. Quarterly.
Journal of Commonwealth Literature. v. 1– . 1965– . Oxford: Hans Zell. Biannual. The December issue has a bibliography of Canadian literature aiming for comprehensiveness and an introductory essay on developments in Canadian literature.

Resources for Feminist Research/Documentation sur la recherche feministe.
   v. 1– . 1979– . Toronto: Ontario Institute for Studies in Education. Quarterly.
University of Toronto Quarterly. v. 1– . 1931– . Toronto: University of Toronto
   Press. Quarterly. The "Letters in Canada" fall issue contains review essays of
   selected titles in the Canadian novel, poetry, drama and theater, English and
   French titles.

Comprehensive Coverage

Bibliographie du Québec. v. 1– . 1968– . Montréal: Bibliothèque Nationale du
   Québec. Monthly with annual cumulations.
*Canadiana: Canada's National Bibliography/La bibliographie nationale du Can-
   ada.* v. 1– . 1950– . Ottawa: Communication Canada (for the National Library
   of Canada). Monthly.

Annual Reviews

Canadian Book Review Annual. v. 1– . 1975– . Toronto: Simon & Pierre. Annual.

Checklists

Acadiensis. v. 1– . 1971– . Fredericton, N.B.: Department of History, University
   of New Brunswick. Biannual. Recent publications relating to the history of the
   Atlantic region.
BC Studies. v. 1– . 1968– . Vancouver: University of British Columbia. Quarterly.
   Bibliography of British Columbia.
Canadian Ethnic Studies/Etudes ethniques au Canada. v. 1– . 1969– . Calgary:
   Research Centre for Canadian Ethnic Studies, University of Calgary.
   Triannually.
Canadian Historical Review. v. 1– . 1920– . Toronto: University of Toronto Press.
   Quarterly. As complete coverage as possible of newly available material useful
   in the study of any aspect of Canadian history.
Histoire sociale/Social History. v. 1– . 1968– . Ottawa: Editions de l'Université
   d'Ottawa. Biannual. A current bibliography on the history of Canadian pop-
   ulation and historical demography in Canada.
ICCS Contact CIEC. v. 1– . 1982– . Ottawa: International Council for Canadian
   Studies. Biannual. Canadian studies: foreign publications and theses.
Journal of Canadian Art History/Annales d'histoire de l'art canadien. v. 1– .
   1974– . Montréal: Concordia University. Biannual. Recent publications on
   Canadian art.
Labour/Le Travail. v. 1– . 1976– . St. John's, Newfoundland: History Depart-
   ment, Memorial University. Biannual. Recent publications in Canadian labor
   history.
Newfoundland Studies v. 1– . 1985– . St. John's, Newfoundland: Department of
   English Language and Literature, Memorial University. Biannual. Selected
   publications and studies related to Newfoundland and Labrador.
Revue d'histoire de l'Amérique française. v. 1– . 1947– . Montréal: Institut
   d'histoire de l'Amérique française. Quarterly.

Core Collections

Cariou, Mavis, Sandra J. Cox and Alvan Bregman. *Canadian Selection: Books and Periodicals for Libraries.* 2nd ed. Toronto: University of Toronto Press, 1985.

Senécal, André. *Canada: A Reader's Guide/Introduction bibliographique.* Ottawa: International Council for Canadian Studies, 1991.

Senécal, André. *A Reader's Guide to Quebec Studies: 1988.* Quebec: Gouvernement du Québec, 1988.

Availability

Canadian Books in Print: Author and Title Index. v. 1– . 1967– . Toronto: University of Toronto Press. Annual; quarterly microfiche editions 1980– .

Canadian Books in Print: Subject Index. v. 1– . 1975– . Toronto: University of Toronto Press. Annual.

Les livres disponibles canadiens de langue française. 1987– . Montreal: Bibliodata. Quarterly hard copy cumulations and fiche copies ten times a year.

Reference

Boivin, Henri-Bernard. *Les Ouvrages de référence du Québec: supplément 1974–1981.* Montréal: Ministère des Affaires culturelles, Bibliothèque Nationale du Québec, 1984.

Bosa, Real. *Les Ouvrages de référence du Québec: bibliographie analytique compilée sous la direction de Real Bosa.* Québec: Ministère des Affaires culturelles du Québec, 1969.

Canadian Library Journal. v. 1– . 1944– . Ottawa: Canadian Library Association. Bimonthly.

Feliciter. v. 1– . 1956– . Ottawa: Canadian Library Association. 10/yr.

Lauzier, Suzanne. *Les Ouvrages de référence du Québec: supplément 1967–1974/ Suzanne Lauzier, Normand Cormier; avec la collaboration de Ghislaine Houle, Yvon-André Lacroix.* Montréal: Bibliothèque Nationale du Québec, 1975.

Papers of the Bibliographical Society of Canada/Cahiers de la Société bibliographique du Canada. v. 1– . 1962– . Toronto: Bibliographical Society of Canada. Biannual.

Ryder, Dorothy. *Canadian Reference Sources: A Selective Guide.* 2nd ed. Ottawa: Canadian Library Association, 1981.

SERIALS

Current

Canadian Magazines for Everyone. 1980– . Toronto: Canadian Magazine Publishers' Association. Annual. (Address: Canadian Magazine Publishers' Association, 2 Stewart Street, Toronto, Ontario, Canada M5V 1H6)

Canadian Serials Directory/Répertoire des publications seriées canadiennes. 3rd ed. Gordon Ripley, ed. Toronto: Reference Press, 1987.

Indexing

Canadian Index. v. 1– . 1993– . Toronto: Micromedia. Monthly with semiannual cumulations.
Canadian Periodical Index. v. 1– . 1928–32; 1938– . Toronto: Info Globe. Monthly with annual cumulations.

News Indexes

Canadian Index. v. 1– . 1993– . Toronto: Micromedia. Monthly with semiannual cumulations.
Index de l'actualité. v. 1– . 1988– . Montréal: Inform II—Microfor. Monthly with annual cumulations.

News Magazines

L'actualité. v. 1– . 1976– . Montréal: Maclean Hunter. 20/yr.
Maclean's. v. 1– . 1905– . Toronto: Maclean Hunter. Weekly.

GOVERNMENT PUBLICATIONS

Current

Gillham, Virginia, comp. "Canada." *Government Publications Review.* v. 1– . 1973– . New York: Pergamon Press. Annual selection.
Government of Canada Publications/Publications du gouvernement du Canada: Quarterly Catalogue trimestriel. 1953– . Ottawa: Canada Communication Group. Quarterly.
Special List of Canadian Government Publications/Liste speciale des publications du gouvernement du Canada. 1969– . Ottawa: Canada Communication Group. Monthly.
Statistics Canada Catalogue. 1930– . Ottawa: Statistics Canada. Annual. (Address: Statistics Canada, Publication Sales, Room 1710, Main Building, Statistics Canada, Ottawa, Ontario, Canada K1A 0T6.)
Weekly Checklist of Canadian Government Publications/Liste hebdomadaire des publications du gouvernement du Canada. 1978– . Ottawa: Canada Communication Group. Weekly.

Indexes

Government of Canada Publications/Publications du gouvernement du Canada: Quarterly Catalogue trimestriel. Ottawa: Canada Communication Group.
Microlog: Canadian Research Index. 1979– . Toronto: Micromedia. Monthly.

CHILDREN AND YOUNG ADULT

Current

CM: A Reviewing Journal of Canadian Materials for Young People. v. 1– . 1971– . Ottawa: Canadian Library Association. Bimonthly.

Children's Book News. v. 1– . 1979– . Toronto: Canadian Children's Book Centre. Quarterly. (Address: Canadian Children's Book Centre, 35 Spadina Road, Toronto, Ontario, Canada M5R 2S9.)

Emergency Librarian. v. 1– . 1973– . Vancouver: Dyad Services. 5/yr.

Lurelu: la seule revue exclusivement consacrée a la littérature québecoise pour la jeunesse. v. 1– . 1978– . Saint Jérome: Association Lurelu. Triannually.

Our Choice. v. 1– . 1978– . Toronto: Canadian Children's Book Centre. Annual. (Address: Canadian Children's Book Centre, 35 Spadina Road, Toronto, Ontario, Canada M5R 2S9.)

Teaching Librarian. v. 1– . 1993– . Toronto: Ontario Library Association Publications. Triannually.

Retrospective

Canadian Children's Literature/Littérature canadienne pour la jeunesse. v. 1– . 1975– . Guelph, Ont.: Canadian Children's Press. Quarterly.

Egoff, Sheila and Judith Saltman. *The New Republic of Childhood: A Critical Guide to Canadian Children's Literature in English.* Toronto: Oxford University Press, 1990.

Gagnon, André and Ann Gagnon, eds. *Canadian Books for Young People/Livres canadiens pour la jeunesse.* 4th ed. Toronto: University of Toronto Press, 1988.

McQuarie, Jane. *Canadian Picture Books: A Subject Guide/Livres d'images canadiens pour enfants: un guide thématique.* Toronto: Reference Press, 1986.

Notable Canadian Children's Books/Un choix de livres canadiens pour la jeunesse. 1973– . Ottawa: National Library of Canada. Irregular.

Too Good to Miss: Classic Canadian Children's Books. Toronto: Canadian Children's Book Centre, 1989. (Address: Canadian Children's Book Centre, 35 Spadina Road, Toronto, Ontario, Canada M5R 2S9.)

SPECIAL FORMATS

Computer Files

CULDAT Canadian Union List of Machine Readable Data Files. Edmonton, Alberta: University of Alberta Data Library. For information and instructions on searching contact the Data Librarian (whose electronic mail address is abombak@vm.ucs.ualberta.ca).

Canadian CD-ROM News. v. 1– . 1987– . Ottawa: Canadian Library CD-ROM Interest Group. Bimonthly.

Database Canada. v. 1– . 1988– . Toronto: Database Canada. Bimonthly.

Directory of Canadian University Data Libraries/Archives. Edmonton, Alberta: University of Alberta Data Library, 1990.

The ESPIAL Canadian Database Directory/Répertoire ESPIAL des bases de données canadiennes. Toronto: Espial Productions, 1990– . Annual.

Roper Center Guide to Canadian Public Opinion Resources. Storrs, Conn.: Roper Center for Public Opinion Research, 1992.

Maps

Parry, R. B. and C. R. Perkins. *World Mapping Today.* London: Butterworths, 1987.

Microforms

See vendor list.

Music

Acquisitions. 1984– . Toronto: Canadian Music Centre. Annual.
Music Directory Canada. 1983– . Toronto: CM Books. Biennial.

Audiovisual

Choix: documentation audiovisuelle. 1978– . [Québec]: Gouvernement du Québec, Ministère de l'éducation, Centrale des bibliothèques. Bimonthly.
DAVID (Documents Audio VIsuels Disponibles). Database available from Services documentaires multimedia, 75 rue de Port-Royal Est, bureau 300, Montréal, Québec, Canada H3L 3T1.
Film/Video Canadiana. v. 1– . 1993– . Ottawa: National Film Board of Canada. Quarterly.
National Film Board of Canada. *Film and Video Catalogue.* 1984– . Montreal: National Film Board of Canada. Irregular.
Visual Media/Médias visuels. v. 1– . 1988– . Etobicoke, Ontario: Ontario Film Association. 5/yr.

Notes

1. English and French, which are the two dominant languages of publication, are considered in this chapter. For publications in other languages see: Ruth Bogusis, *Checklist of Canadian Ethnic Serials* (Ottawa: National Library of Canada, 1981); Andrew Gregorovich, *Canadian Ethnic Press Bibliography* (Toronto: Canadian Multilingual Press Federation, 1991); Jean-Michel Lacroix, *Anatomie de la Presse Ethnique au Canada* (Bordeaux: Presses Universitaires de Bordeaux, 1988); John Miska, *Ethnic and Native Canadian Literature: A Bibliography* (Toronto: University of Toronto Press, 1990); and Judy Young, "Some Thoughts about the Present State of Bibliography in the Area of Canadian Ethnic Studies," *Canadian Issues* 4 (1982): 38–47.
2. For this chapter the National Library's definition is adopted. Variations are noted when they are not immediately apparent from the scope of the work being discussed.
3. Royal Commission on Book Publishing, *Canadian Publishers and Canadian Publishing* (Toronto: Queen's Printer, 1973), and *Royal Commission on Book Publishing: Background Papers* (Toronto: Queen's Printer, 1972). A valuable overview of the Canadian book trade appears in Frances G. Halpenny, "From Author to Reader," *Literary History of Canada,* 2nd ed. (Toronto: University of Toronto Press, 1990), vol. 4, pp. 385–404.

4. Statistics Canada, *Book Publishing 1990–91* (Ottawa: Statistics Canada, 1991), p. 10.
5. Ibid., p. 47.
6. Ibid., pp. 15, 16, 17.
7. Their address is Book and Periodical Council, 35 Spadina Road, Toronto, Ontario, Canada M5R 2S9. An informative overview of the trade can be gained from Frances G. Halpenny, "From Author to Reader," *Literary History of Canada,* 2nd ed. (Toronto: University of Toronto Press, 1990), vol. 4, pp. 385–404.
8. Editorial statement, *Quill & Quire* 58 (March, 1992): 4.
9. In this context the *Directory of Canadian Associations* provides information on many groups such as the League of Canadian Poets, professional associations in all fields, the Canadian Country Music Association, and national, regional, and local historical societies. Brian Land, ed., *Directory of Associations in Canada/Répertoire des associations du Canada,* 12th ed. (Toronto: Micromedia, 1991). For the selector outside of Canada the biennial *International Directory to Canadian Studies/Répertoire international des etudes canadiennes* (Ottawa: International Council for Canadian Studies) will locate the Canadian Studies Association in their own country.
10. Judith Turnbull and Richard Bingham, eds., "Spring Announcements," *Quill & Quire* 58 (March, 1992): 21.
11. Ibid.
12. National Library of Canada, *Forthcoming Books/Livres à paraître* 1 (March, 1992).
13. This information was generously provided in a phone conversation with the director of the National CIP program at the National Library of Canada.
14. The catalog should be requested from the Association for the Export of Canadian Books, 504-1 rue Nicholas, Ottawa, Ontario, Canada K1N 7B7.
15. These catalogs can be requested from: Genny Urquhart, Canadian Book Information Center, 260 King Street East, Toronto, Ontario, Canada M5A 1K3.
16. The catalog can be ordered from: Playwrights Union of Canada, 54 Wolseley Street, 2nd Floor, Toronto, Ontario, Canada M5T 1A5.
17. The address of InBook is P.O. Box 120261, East Haven, CT 06512. The address of the Literary Press Group is 260 King Street East, Toronto, Ontario, Canada M5A 1K3.
18. Although not as extensive, the Association for Canadian Studies' *Bulletin* is also useful for Canadian studies titles. The full title is *ACS Newsletter/ Bulletin de l'AEC.*
19. André Senécal, *Canada: A Reader's Guide/Introduction bibliographique* (Ottawa: International Council for Canadian Studies, 1991), pp. 352–69.
20. "Preface," *Canadiana,* November, 1991, p. iv.
21. As a result of recent changes in deposit requirements, *Canadiana* will have a fuller coverage of videos and CD-ROMs in 1993.
22. Subscriptions are entered through Canada Communication Group/ Publishing, Supply and Services Canada, Ottawa, Ontario, Canada K1A 0S9.

23. Senécal, p. xiii.

24. The addresses of these firms are given in appendix A.

25. A bibliography entitled *Canada* (Santa Barbara, Calif.: Clio Press, 1990) by Ernest Ingles will serve in many instances to update Ryder's work. Another work (currently being compiled) that will be very useful when it appears is the third edition of the *Bibliography of Canadian Bibliographies.*

26. Mary Bond, "Guide to Canadian Reference Sources: A Progress Report," *National Library News* 23, no. 1 (January, 1991): 7.

27. For an extensive discussion of the bibliographical tools for Canadian periodicals and newspapers see H. Komorous, "Reference Sources for Canadian Periodicals and Newspapers," *Reference Librarian* 27/28 (1990): 331–45.

28. R. G. Fischer and R. E. Brundin, "Northern Exposure: Thirteen Publications That Will Broaden Our Perception and Understanding of Canada," *Library Journal* 114 (May 1, 1989): 51–55.

29. The address of the Association is 2 Stewart Street, Toronto, Ontario, Canada M5V 1H6.

30. Beginning in 1993 the *Canadian Index* consolidates the *Canadian Business Index,* the *Canadian Magazine Index,* and the *Canadian News Index.*

31. Brian Land, "Government Publications: A Description and Guide to the Use of Canadian Government Publications," in Paul Fox and Graham White, *Politics: Canada* (Toronto: McGraw-Hill Ryerson Ltd., 1991), 527–51; Olga Bishop, *Canadian Official Publications* (Oxford: Pergamon, 1981).

32. A subscription to the *Checklist* should be sent to Canada Communication Group, Publishing Division, Ottawa, Ontario, Canada K1A 0S9.

33. Available from Publication Sales, Room 1710, Main Building, Statistics Canada, Ottawa, Ontario, Canada K1A 0T6.

34. Land, pp. 545–50.

35. Louise Carpentier, "The Acquisition of the Publications of the Quebec Government," *Government Publications Review* 19 (May-June, 1992): 257–68. Carpentier has also published annual reviews of Quebec government publications in microform and non-print in *Microform Review* since 1988. The latest article is "Quebec Government Publications in Microform and Other Non-Print Formats: Past, Present, and Future Years," *Microform Review* 19, no. 4 (Fall, 1990): 174–80.

36. Virginia Gillham, "Canada," *Government Publications Review* 19 (Nov.-Dec., 1992): 605–29.

37. This pamphlet is available from Canada Communication Group, Publishing, Ottawa, Ontario, Canada K1A 0S9.

38. All the articles have been written by Mary Luebbe. The latest one is "1990 Survey of Canadian Government Documents Micropublishers," *Microform Review* 19 (Fall, 1990): 166–73.

39. The address for the Canadian Children's Book Centre is 35 Spadina Road, Toronto, Ontario, Canada M5R 2S9.

40. The address for Communication—jeunesse is 964 rue Cherrier, Montreal, Quebec, Canada H2L 1H7.

41. *CM* 4 (January, 1991): 4.

42. Anna Altmann, Sheila Bertram, and Mary Field, "Reviews of Young Adult Books in Canadian Reviewing Serials," *Canadian Library Journal* 48, no. 6 (December, 1991): 385–91. In their comparison of five Canadian reviewing serials, *CM* had by far the largest number of reviews.

43. Another Quebec review of literature for youth that has less substantial reviews and is not limited to Quebec publications is *Des Livres et des Jeunes,* v. 1, no. 1, November, 1978– (Sherbrooke, Québec: Association canadienne pour l'avancement de la litterature de jeunesse).

44. The *Hornbook* also runs a regular column on Canadian children's literature called "News from the North." Although the reviews are more in depth, the number of titles reviewed is so small (3 to 5) that it has very limited use for acquisitions.

45. Ronald Jobe and Irene Aubrey, "Canadian Books for Children," *Booklist* 85 (June 15, 1990): 1999–2002. Earlier lists appear in the November 15, 1987, December 1, 1986, May 1, 1985, and January 15, 1984, issues of *Booklist*.

46. *Canadian Books for Young People/Livres canadiens pour la jeunesse* (Toronto: University of Toronto Press, 1988).

47. Elspeth Ross, "Children's Books on Contemporary North American Indian/Native/Metis Life: A Selected Bibliography of Books and Professional Reading," *Canadian Children's Literature* 61 (1991): 29–43; and Joan Weller, "Canadian English Language Juvenile Periodicals: An Historical Overview 1847–1990," *Canadian Children's Literature* 59 (1990): 38–69.

48. *Gale Directory of Databases: Volume 1: Online Databases* (Detroit: Gale Research, 1993).

49. *Gale Directory of Online Databases: Volume 2: CD-ROM, Diskette, Magnetic Tape, Handheld, and Batch Access Database Products* (Detroit: Gale Research, 1993).

50. The full address of the company is SDM Inc. (Services documentaires multimédia Inc.), 75 rue de Port-Royal Est, bureau 300, Montréal, Québec, Canada H3L 3T1.

51. Bonnie Campbell, "CD-ROM Publishing in Canada," *Laserdisk Professional* 2, no. 5 (September, 1989): 31–34; Paul Nicholls, "Optical Options: Canadian Content on CD-ROM," *Database Canada* 2, no. 4 (June, 1990): 15; and Carol Cook, "Canadian Content Sparse on CD-ROM," *Information Today* 8, no. 7 (July-August, 1991): 19–20.

52. For the truly dedicated statistics collector *The Daily,* a publication of Statistics Canada, lists data availability on a daily basis.

53. For more information contact Canada Institute for Scientific and Technical Information, National Research Council Canada, Ottawa, Ontario, Canada K1A 0S2, telephone 613-993-1210.

54. The eleven newspapers are: the *Calgary Herald,* the *Daily News* (Halifax), the *Edmonton Journal,* the *Gazette* (Montreal), *Kitchener-Waterloo Record, La Presse,* the *Ottawa Citizen,* the *Province* (Vancouver), the *Toronto Star,* the *Vancouver Sun,* and the *Windsor Star.*

55. SDM's address is 75 rue de Port-Royal Est, bureau 300, Montréal, Québec, Canada H3L 3T1 with the phone number 514-382-0895.

56. Jacqueline Halupka, "Online in Canada," *Online* 13, no. 6 (November, 1989): 123–27; Susan Merry, Cynthea Penman and Philomena Pun, "The Canadian Connection: Business Online," *Database* 12, no. 5 (October, 1989): 15–27; Ulla De Stricker and Jane Dysart, *Business Online* (Toronto: John Wiley, 1989).

57. The full mail address for inquiries is Anna Bombak, Data Librarian, 352 General Services Building, University Computing Systems, University of Alberta, Edmonton, Alberta, Canada T6G 2H1.

58. The *Directory* published by the University of Alberta Data Library in 1990 is available from them at University Computing Systems, 415 Cameron Library, University of Alberta Library, Edmonton, Alberta, Canada T6G 2J8.

59. The address for the ICPSR is Inter-University Consortium for Political and Social Research, Institute for Social Research, P.O. Box 1248, Ann Arbor, MI 48106, and the address for the Roper Center is P.O. Box 440, Storrs, CT 06268; telephone 203-486-4440.

60. "Canada," in *World Mapping Today,* by R. B. Parry and C. R. Perkins (London: Butterworths, 1987), pp. 166–78.

61. The address is: 615 Booth Street, Ottawa, Ontario, Canada K1A 0E9 of the Department of Energy, Mines and Resources.

62. *Microform Marketplace: MMP; An International Directory of Micropublishing* (Munich: Saur, 1991), pp. 159–60.

63. Suzanne Cates Dodson, *Microform Research Collections* (Westport, Conn.: Meckler, 1984), pp. 627–28.

64. All theses microfilmed by the National Library appear in *Canadiana,* and the National Library also publishes semiannually with five-year cumulations *Canadian Theses (Microfiche),* a microfiche bibliography of all Canadian master's and doctoral theses as well as foreign theses of Canadian authorship or interest. Two other National Library titles of interest are *Doctoral Research on Canada and Canadians 1884–1983* (Ottawa: National Library of Canada, 1986) and *Theses in Canada: A Bibliographic Guide* (Ottawa: National Library of Canada, 1986).

65. Canadian theses microfilmed before February, 1991, should be ordered from Micromedia Limited; since February, 1991, Micromedia Limited is responsible for Canadian sales and UMI is the international sales agent. To order theses from Micromedia Limited write Micromedia Limited, 165 Hôtel de Ville, Hull, Québec, Canada J8X 3X2, or telephone 819-770-9928. To order from UMI phone 800-521-0600, ext. 870.

66. Joan Colquhoun, "Bibliographic Control of Canadian Music Materials," *Fontes Artis Musicae* 34, no. 4 (Oct.-Dec., 1987): 256.

67. The national office of the Centre is located at 20 St. Joseph Street, Toronto, Ontario, Canada M4Y 1J9. The Centre also has regional offices in Montreal, Calgary, and Vancouver. For a history of the Centre see Karen Keiser and Mark Hand, "The Canadian Music Centre: A History," *Fontes Artis Musicae* 34, no. 4 (Oct.-Dec., 1987): 216–23; and Mireille Gagne, "Le Centre de la Musique canadienne au Québec, une brève description," *Fontes Artis Musicae* 34, no. 4 (Oct.-Dec., 1987): 223–26.

68. The *ACS Newsletter/Bulletin de l'AEC* 13, no. 4 (Winter, 1991–92) is devoted to audiovisual resources for Canadian studies and contains a number of articles worth reading for the selector who wants further information.

69. Donald Bidd, "The National Film Board of Canada: A Major Resource for Canadian Studies," *ACS Newsletter/Bulletin de l'AEC* 13, no. 4 (Winter, 1991–92): 10.

70. The CD-ROM can be ordered from: OPTIM Corporation, 150 Isabella Street, Second Floor, Ottawa, Ontario, Canada K1S 1V7.

71. Orders for the 1987–88 edition and earlier years back to 1980 can be placed with: National Film Board of Canada, Customer Services D10, Film/Video Canadiana, P.O. Box 6100, Station A, Montreal, Quebec, Canada H3C 3H5.

72. A complete filmography of all the English and French productions of the NFB was published in 1991. This work contains many titles which are no longer commercially distributed. See: National Film Board of Canada, *The NFB Film Guide: The Productions of the National Film Board of Canada from 1939 to 1989,* National Film Board of Canada, 1991.

73. The catalogs can be ordered from the following address: National Film Board of Canada, Customer Services, P.O. Box 6100, Station A, Montréal, Québec, Canada H3C 3H5. The U.S. and international catalogs are free of charge.

74. The addresses of the international offices are as follows: 1251 Avenue of the Americas, 16th Floor, New York, NY 10021, U.S.A.; 1 Grosvenor Square, London, England, W1X 0AB, U.K.; 15 rue de Berri, 75008 Paris, France; International Program, P.O. Box 6100, Montréal, Québec, Canada H3C 3H5.

75. The address is as follows: Canadian Film Distribution Center, State University of New York at Plattsburgh, Feinberg Library, Rooms 124-128, Plattsburgh, NY 12901-2637.

76. Requests for the catalogs should be sent to the Canadian Filmmakers Distribution Centre, 67A Portland Street, Toronto, Ontario, Canada M5V 2M9.

77. The 1993 edition can be ordered from: Liz Avison, Library Consultant, 61 Mann Avenue, Toronto, Ontario, Canada M4S 2Y2.

78. Requests for CBC catalogs should be sent to CBC Educational Sales at one of the following three addresses: Box 500, Station A, Toronto, Ontario, Canada M5W 1E6; 43 Great Titchfield St., London, W1P 8DD, U.K.; Suite 5507, Empire State Bldg., 350 5th Avenue, New York, NY 10118, U.S.A. CTV catalogs are available from: CTV Television Network Ltd., Program Sales, 42 Charles Street East, Toronto, Ontario, Canada M4Y 1T5. TVO catalogues are available from: TVO Marketing, Box 200, Station Q, Toronto, Ontario, Canada M4T 2T1.

79. Ernest J. Dick, *Guide to CBC Sources at the Public Archives* (Ottawa: Public Archives of Canada, 1987) and *Canadian Feature Film Index, 1913–1985/ Index des films canadiens de long métrage,* ed. D. J. Turner and Micheline Morisset (Ottawa: Public Archives, National Film, Television, and Sound Archives, 1987). A discussion of the National Archives' collection can be found in Jana Vosikovska, "Canadian Audio-Visual Heritage and the National Archives of Canada," *ACS Newsletter* 13, no. 4 (Winter, 1991–92): 14–16.

80. The respective addresses are: McIntyre Media Ltd., 30 Kelfield Street, Rexdale, Ontario, Canada M9W 5A2 and Bourdon Audiovisuel Inc., 5215 Berri Street, Montréal, Québec, Canada H2J 2S4.

81. All these products are available from: Services documentaires multimédia (SDM) inc., 75 rue de Port-Royal Est, bureau 300, Montréal, Québec, Canada H3L 3T1.

82. A brief description of these guides appears in Louise Carpentier, "The Acquisition of the Publications of the Quebec Government," *Government Publications Review* 19, no. 3 (May-June, 1992): 264–65. For more complete information write to SDM (see note 81).

83. The *Directory* can be obtained from the Antiquarian Booksellers' Association of Canada, P.O. Box 323, Victoria Station, Montréal, Québec, Canada H3Z 2V8. A more extensive list of Quebec booksellers can be obtained from the Confrérie de la Librairie Ancienne du Québec, C.P. 1056, Succ. C, Montréal, Québec, Canada H2L 4V3.

TASMAN SEA

COOK
STRAIT

PACIFIC OCEAN

NEW ZEALAND

Murray S. Martin

While New Zealand is a small, isolated country in the South Pacific, its history and geography have combined to make it a fascinating example of the gradual combining of European and Polynesian (Maori) cultural heritages. It is also a New World country, dependent on third world trade. These oppositions lend world importance to local publications.

The librarian considering collecting New Zealand materials has to decide the place they will fill within the library's total collection. If the object is to support New Zealand studies, the goal will be to develop a well-rounded collection to the level that fits the library goals. If, instead, the goal is to have materials relating to individual subjects, then a more selective approach can be taken. In either case, it may prove helpful to set up an approval plan or to arrange with a dealer or dealers to send information for selection. Several of the dealers listed in appendix D will provide approval plans based on library profiles. Some also mail news-letters or releases about specific books, from which selections can be made. Both methods have the advantage of being monitored on the spot from local information that avoids the long delays inherent in commu-nication with a far distant land. Direct selection from bibliographic or review sources may prove counterproductive, since many print runs are short and the required materials may be out of print. The agreements surrounding New Zealand publishing also work against easy access within the United States, and many needed books will be more easily purchased from British sources. In addition, many works relating to New Zealand are first published (or co-published) in other countries, most notably in Britain, but often in Australia or the United States. Historical ties with Britain often mean that New Zealand authors will seek out a British publisher to get wider distribution. Australian publishers or institutions frequently publish materials that cover New Zealand or that are within their field of interest. University presses in New Zealand often have co-publishing arrrangements with U.S. institutions. This can mean that approval plans or blanket orders will turn up duplicates. It also means that attention has to be paid to reviewing journals in other countries, and that secondhand materials can show up in a variety of locations.

Public libraries may need more popular material or may need to support a strong local interest, either business or trade oriented, particularly on the Pacific coast, or may simply need material on specific topics. In addition, they are more likely to be interested in children's books. Except in the largest libraries, these goals can best be met by specific orders, either through vendors or direct to the publisher or publisher's representative in the United States.

Geographical Description

Often referred to as the Antipodes, i.e., of England but actually of Spain, New Zealand consists of two principal islands, the North and the South islands (local usage incorporates the articles), one large offshore island, Stewart Island, and numerous other islands and island groups. Other territories include the Antipodes, Auckland, Bounty, Chatham and Kermadec islands. Historical links are maintained with the Cook Islands, Rarotonga, Tokelau, and Western Samoa, while New Zealand's claim to a segment of the Antarctic gives it an interest in the fate of that continent. This large spread, from the equator to the South Pole, has given New Zealand an enduring geopolitical interest.

New Zealand's Pakeha (white) population is mostly of British origin, although several other European nations are represented, and a number of idealistic colonies were founded in the second half of the nineteenth century.[1] The first inhabitants were the Maori (there is some suggestion of earlier occupation but the record is by no means clear), a Polynesian people who arrived by sea about a thousand years ago. Recently there has been substantial immigration from the Pacific Islands, and Auckland in particular has settlers from most of the islands. There was some Chinese immigration during the gold rush era in the middle of the nineteenth century, and some other Asian communities are represented. At various times New Zealand accepted limited numbers of refugees (for example, after the invasion of Hungary or the end of the Vietnam War), but these have not changed greatly the British and northern European domination in numbers.

New Zealand is located between 34° and 47° south of the equator, and 166° and 179° east, and has a climate without great temperature variations. Its relationship to the international date line causes both geographical and historical oddities. It is claimed that the first light of the new day falls on the summit of Mount Hikurangi, near East Cape, while New Zealand, because of this difference, actually declared war on Germany on September 3, 1939, before Great Britain.

New Zealand was part of Gondwanaland, probably located between the Australian and Antarctic segments of that landmass. It has been separated for more than 60 million years, which has ensured a unique biota. While most people think first of the kiwi as representing New Zealand, there are many other endemic plants and animals. In generic terms the flora has a higher proportion of endemic species than anywhere else in the world. The native fauna is undoubtedly unique, not perhaps as visibly as that of Australia, but in that it is principally an avifauna (birds). There are only two native mammals (bats), three reptiles including the tuatara, and one native frog. Many of the native birds are flightless, as was the now extinct moa, and others are but poor fliers since they had no predators to contend with. The special nature of New Zealand flora and fauna makes it of great interest to biologists and botanists, and it is covered in an extensive literature.

The introduction of animals from other lands, whether intentional or accidental, has greatly changed the balance. It is claimed that less than ten square miles of the original forest remains unchanged from the predations of deer, opossums, rats, goats, and rabbits. The last-named resulted in a unique local government authority network, the Rabbit Boards, which were charged with exterminating this pest. The gradual elimination of native habitat over most of the country, to promote the agriculture which has become a hallmark, has further weakened native wildlife. The history of acclimatization has not been a good one. It does, however, provide an instructive view of one side of imperialism.[2]

Distance from its principal markets has caused New Zealand agriculture to develop in a distinctive manner, since all products, until recently, have had to contend with a shipping period of six to eight weeks. It has, as a result, become a highly organized business, though not in the same way as, say, the United States. Dairy farming, however, has developed a whole chain of surrounding industry that helps give the country a distinctive appearance. There can be few other places where farm production is so much a part of the national image. Overseas markets still account for a very large part of the gross national product, and the New Zealand economy has been more affected by changes in tariffs and trade patterns than almost any other. Fluctuations in the prices of primary products result directly in the booms and busts that have characterized New Zealand's economic history.

The early history of the country has been one of despoliation of the landscape, as forests were destroyed to make way for farms, and the erosion consequent on the introduction of high country animals has endangered even non-farm land. The beauty of even this changed landscape, with its mountains, glaciers, beaches, volcanoes, lakes, rivers, and fiords, has become a major tourist attraction. It has also become the focus of many preservation societies. There are, at last count, thirteen National Parks covering more than 240 million acres, about one-tenth of the entire country, three maritime parks, many national forests, and numerous local reserves.[3] New Zealand also has several areas of world heritage standard, some formally so recognized. Currently there is great controversy over the government decision to spin off most of its environmental responsibilities, particularly over the creation of crown corporations to manage the forests and other crown lands. Despite the existence of a Ministry of Conservation and numerous advisory bodies, many New Zealanders are apprehensive lest their natural heritage be further despoiled. Such concerns have been reflected in writing by local authors (and visitors) for many years and this concern can be expected to continue. Kipling's words about Auckland—"last, loneliest, loveliest, apart"—have become more than an expression of sentimental enthusiasm as New Zealanders strive to preserve the two latter qualities in a world changed completely by the conquering of the first two.

Historical Background and Current Trends

Human settlement began in New Zealand roughly one thousand years ago with the advent of the first Maori from somewhere in the central Pacific. Although the traditions surrounding the demi-god Maui, who fished New Zealand from the sea, the first explorers Kupe and Toi, and the Great Fleet of seven canoes, in which came the progenitors of all present-day Maori, are now in dispute, they remain the foundation of *Maoritanga* (things Maori). The Maori were basically hunters, fishers, and gatherers but practiced a limited kind of agriculture. Individual holding of land was unknown and even tribal ownership tended to be associational, relating to hunting, fishing, and sacred areas. Tribal relationships were not always cordial, and warfare was almost an occupation.

Genealogy and kinship patterns were vitally important. The *whaka-papa* (genealogies) were memorized and most social gatherings required the establishment of relationships via family history. The religious traditions are now somewhat uncertain, most Maori having converted to Christianity or to local variations. They have a rich heritage of myth, story, and song, but, since the Maori had not developed a written language, these were oral, passed down generation to generation by the *tohungas* (the priestly class) and the *rangatira* (the chiefly class). Written versions prepared by missionaries, government officials, and anthropologists have almost certainly Europeanized much of their content.[4] The resurgence of Maori pride in their heritage, which may be one of the most successful recoveries of a colonized native people anywhere, has recently been accompanied by a renewed interest on the part of the Pakeha.

The first European to "discover" New Zealand was Abel Janszoon Tasman, sailing from Batavia in 1642 on behalf of the Dutch East India Company. His discovery and mapping of the west coast did not prompt further exploration until the late eighteenth century when France and Britain were competing to control the trade and commerce of the world. Captain James Cook was the first (1769) to circumnavigate New Zealand completely, thus placing it firmly on the world map and replacing the mythical Terra Australis, mostly with open ocean. He spent some time in New Zealand as part of his three voyages. This resulted in the first extensive reports on the Maori, whom he greatly admired. His journals include many references, and the illustrations that accompanied the written versions introduced a new world to enlightenment Europe. He also seems to suggest an awareness that the Pacific would never be the same again.[5] There is extensive Cook literature, which includes many items appropriate for a New Zealand collection. Many of the early editions are now very expensive. The early explorers noted the close similarities between Maori and the languages of the various Pacific Islanders and were impressed that apparently primitive peoples could have spread over so large a part of the earth.

Wider European contact followed the founding of a penal colony at Botany Bay in New South Wales in 1788 and the growth of whaling and sealing in the Pacific, activities in which the United States played a prominent role during the Napoleonic Wars.[6] There were several temporary and some permanent settlements by Europeans engaged in whaling and sawmilling. The first mission was established from Australia under the leadership of Samuel Marsden, who held the first Christian religious service on Christmas Day, 1814. The church presence was more than counterbalanced by the lawless settlers and whalers who made the town of Kororareka (now known as Russell) the "Hellhole of the Pacific." An attempt to impose law and order by the introduction of a

British resident (James Busby) in 1838 did not work out and Britain, somewhat reluctantly, sent Captain Hobson to proclaim British sovereignty in 1840.[7]

Direct British settlement was almost contemporaneous. In fact the first Wakefield-inspired settlers set out before the signing of the Treaty of Waitangi.[8] Wellington (1840) and later settlements in Nelson, Wanganui, and New Plymouth were founded, often by members of the Wakefield family, in accordance with his principles of establishing a cross section of British society, with land sold at a sufficient price to preempt purchase by the improvident. Later settlers came to Canterbury and Otago, with the support and blessing of the Anglican and Presbyterian churches, respectively. These were soon overwhelmed by the influx of other free settlers and migrants from Australia. The gold rushes expanded the population dramatically. As with whaling and sealing, the gold rush era included an American presence, with traffic between Australia, New Zealand, and California.

Almost from the beginning there was conflict with the Maori, principally over land. Despite the supposed guarantees in the Treaty of Waitangi (1840), much land was quickly alienated and a shilly-shallying government policy both in Auckland and in London did little to resolve the disputes.[9] A series of land wars between 1844 and 1872 secured Pakeha dominance, but at a severe price. Economic development of the North Island was held back, and the costs of the war prevented other government investment. The Maori declined in numbers and spirit and were expected to die out by the end of the nineteenth century. A cultural renaissance, beginning with agriculture and health in the early twentieth century and later extending to all things Maori, reversed the trend. Today, out of a total population of about 3.4 million, there are more than 400,000 who identify themselves as Maori, and many more with differing degrees of Maori ancestry. They are mainly located in the North Island and in some parts form a majority of the population.

New Zealand has claimed an outstanding record of racial harmony. While discrimination is illegal, the historic record confirms the view of the Maori as second-class citizens, despite their having gained the right to vote before Pakeha women. Economically they have continued to exist in a depressed economic state, and are only gradually finding equal opportunity. An official policy of integration in fact suppressed Maoridom, and has only recently been reversed. For too long it was, for example, forbidden to teach or use the Maori language in schools, and Maori studies have only been accepted into curricula in very recent years.

The Maori are, however, nothing if not resilient, and have used their Maori members of parliament, their various tribal committees, and the Land Courts to fight back. Building on some of the more constructive work of the Department of Maori Affairs, recent administrations have moved to promote equality. New Zealand is now officially bilingual, using Maori and English, the former somewhat less than universally, and the Treaty of Waitangi Tribunal Act (1975 and amendments) set up a tribunal to hear Maori complaints relating to land sales, and hunting and fishing rights. Its decisions so far have been favorable to Maori interests.

The approach of the sesquicentennial year in 1990 also prompted much soul-searching about race relations in New Zealand. In fact the government did not so much celebrate 150 years of settlement as promote discussion of New Zealand's future. Maori and Pakeha writers have given these ideas expression and have encouraged a genuine desire to create a new culture founded on two heritages. This has had a substantial effect on local writing, causing both acclaim and concern.[10] Libraries, too, have shown leadership in promoting multiculturalism.[11] What lasting effects these efforts will have remains to be seen, but it is clear that Maori opinion now has more influence than it has had in a long time. The extensive literature on race relations and history is of great interest to other countries now looking at their own ethnic diversity.

The Dominion of New Zealand is an independent monarchical member of the Commonwealth of Nations. The monarch is the current Queen or King of Great Britain, represented in New Zealand by a Governor-General, with much more restricted powers than the counterpart in Australia. In common with the other "Old Dominions," New Zealand has departed from the tradition of appointing British peers or generals.[12] Recent Governors-General have included an ex-Prime Minister, Sir Keith Holyoke, an Archbishop, Sir Paul Reeves, and an ex-mayor of Auckland, Dame Catherine Tizard. New Zealand is unique in having a unicameral legislature—the House of Representatives. In a parliamentary democracy that means that the current Prime Minister, as leader of the party in power, is virtually free of constraint and there has been some concern at the possibilities of dictatorship.[13] There is no provision for judicial review of legislation. There are two major political parties, Labour and National (conservative), and electoral history seems to show a kind of pendulum effect by which each replaces the other after a time.[14] To balance this central political power there is an ombudsman or Parliamentary Commissioner for Investigation, who, with colleagues added by later legislation, may investigate public complaints against the government bureaucracy at national and local levels. There is a bewildering array of local territorial and ad hoc authorities, although recent legislation has reduced their numbers drastically.

The franchise is universal for those over eighteen years of age. Women were granted the vote in 1893, a world first. The Maori have had four Maori electorates since the middle of the nineteenth century, although the choice of where to vote may now be exercised on a personal basis. Because the Maori have generally supported the Ratana Church-Labour Party alliance, the National Party when in power has mostly had to appoint non-Maori to the post of Minister of Maori Affairs. On occasion, however, Maori Members of Parliament have been elected to represent non-Maori electorates.

Government has always had a wide influence on New Zealand affairs. Broadcasting, education, health, power generation, railways, roads and forests have been government owned and operated. Of recent years some operations have been privatized and others transferred to crown corporations or to government-owned enterprises. In addition there has been a move to devolve responsibility to local authorities. The trend continues, regardless of the political party in power, and has caused fears that the government may be giving up legitimate public concerns, especially true in matters concerning the environment.

From World War II on, New Zealand found itself in a new setting, where the United States came to replace the United Kingdom as its principal ally. This was reinforced by Britain's joining the European Common Market, which disrupted already tenuous trade patterns. New Zealand had always been a loyal follower of British leadership and felt deserted. It had taken New Zealand a long time officially to adopt the trappings of independence and now the country felt alone in a hostile world. This does not contradict the fact that New Zealand has always felt able to oppose actions by the Great Powers[15] and that it takes an active role in Pacific affairs. The latter interest finally brought conflict with the United States over nuclear weapons. All political parties support the policy that keeps New Zealand nuclear-free and they also support the nuclear-free zone in the South Pacific. Equally, although New Zealand had aways supported Britain in her wars, and did the same in Korea and Vietnam for the Americans, she felt free to differ and was one of the first countries to establish regular diplomatic relations with Communist China. These decisions reflect an informed public opinion, which has always been an important factor in New Zealand politics.[16]

LITERACY

New Zealand has always prided itself on a high level of literacy and continues to promote reading skills.[17] In part this is a carryover from the high ideals of the early colonists, in part a reaction to the fact that New Zealand is isolated and reading provides ready access to the rest of the world. The level of reading will, naturally, vary greatly. It has been estimated that through the middle of the twentieth century, the critical audience for New Zealand writing itself could be numbered only in the hundreds. Nevertheless reading continues at a high level, only slightly lowered by the advent of videos and television. The estimate is that New Zealanders spend $60 per head per year on books. The high level of literacy sustains a wide variety of publishing on local topics. In addition the school reading program has resulted in the publication of several handbooks and kits, which have been adopted by schools in other countries, including the United States.

LIBRARIES

Most New Zealand towns have libraries and bookstores, even if only small. The first library, the Wellington Athenaeum, was established in 1841. There are now more than 170 public library systems and 650 community libraries. Those in the main centers—Auckland, Wellington, Christchurch, and Dunedin—are large and have significant special collections, but most are comparatively small. These have been supplemented by the National Library of New Zealand's Extension Division. Recent action by the government, following a report by Price Waterhouse, has curtailed these services substantially and the three district centers have been dismantled.[18] The School Library Service will continue its work in supporting libraries in primary and district high schools but not by making direct loans. These represent the most recent steps in a long history of library development, dating from the 1930s when the Carnegie Corporation of New York provided funds to reinvigorate libraries, and the first Labour Government, through the Minister of Education, Peter Fraser, made a commitment to nationwide access to libraries.[19]

The National Library of New Zealand (Te Puna Matauranga o Aotearoa) was created in 1965. The collections from the beginning were conceived as the library of last resort for the country, and the NLNZ is the center of the national interlibrary lending system, known locally as "interloan." It supports the National Union Catalog, now computerized as the New Zealand Bibliographical Network (NZBN). It produces the *New Zealand National Bibliography* and *Index New Zealand,* both online and in microformat.

The Alexander Turnbull Library (part of the NZNL) has a special status and was developed from the personal collection that Alexander Turnbull willed to the nation after his death in 1918. It is a national research library responsible for the preservation of the New Zealand literary heritage, and also has significant collections on the Pacific, early printed books, and John Milton. The National Archives are separate but often share responsibilities with the Turnbull. In addition there are also massive files of microfilmed newspapers.

The Carnegie Corporation also assisted university libraries in upgrading their collections and practices. Formerly constituent colleges of the

University of New Zealand, they are now independent. There are seven universities: the University of Auckland, the University of the Waikato (Hamilton), Massey University (Palmerston North), Victoria University of Wellington, Canterbury University (Christchurch), Lincoln University (formerly an agricultural college), and the University of Otago (Dunedin). Massey University has a unique role in that it provides distance education to the whole country. Several books and articles have been written about this service. All libraries have significant collections and specializations that reflect their academic programs.[20] In a style common in New Zealand they cooperate to ensure broad disciplinary coverage without wasting funds.

Of special interest is the Hocken Library (University of Otago), begun with the bequest of another early bibliophile, Dr. T. M. Hocken. Its aim is to have everything published in and about New Zealand, together with a strong representation of Pacific materials. It now has more than 140,000 volumes, together with manuscripts and archives, and more than 6,000 original paintings. There are also several teacher's training colleges and polytechnic institutes. The theological colleges and seminaries have libraries that include manuscripts, archives, rare books, and books on early New Zealand and the Pacific. These smaller libraries often contain important material.[21] Victoria University of Wellington houses the New Zealand Library School, which was formerly part of the National Library Service.

Education, which has always been a government concern, has been undergoing dramatic changes. Instead of education boards, there are now individually contracted schools with their own boards of governors, and parents may opt for private schools or teach their own children. The same kind of program is proposed for the universities. It remains to be seen what effect this will have on the formerly highly structured educational system and on libraries. A recent description by Gwen Gawaith suggests that most school libraries are poorly organized and not truly in a position to cope with the changes in the School Library Service.[22]

There are more than three hundred special libraries, including corporations, societies, museums, local government authorities, and professional associations. Of particular importance are the libraries formerly part of the Department of Scientific and Industrial Research (DSIR), which had sizeable collections covering every aspect of science and technology. The various DSIR units have been privatized as Crown Research Institutes and the fate of their libraries and of any cooperative endeavors is somewhat uncertain.[23] The DSIR, together with the NLNZ, sponsored SATIS (Scientific and Technical Information Services), an on-line database, and there are several other databases such as SIRIS, which since 1980 has provided a keyword index to abstracts of New Zealand sci-tech publications. There are important collections also in the various museums that have a great deal of New Zealand-related material.

With the decline in library budgets in the United States, knowledge of collections in New Zealand libraries can help bolster local collections through interlibrary loan and document delivery. Dollar shortages in New Zealand also encourage the setting up of publication exchange programs.

Publishing and Writing

The beginning of publishing in New Zealand is closely linked to official and religious endeavors. While the first book actually printed and published in New Zealand was a Maori translation of St Paul's Epistles to the Ephesians and the Philippians by William Williams at the Paihia Mission Station in 1835, earlier books had been produced in England and Australia for Church Missionary Society distribution in New Zealand.[24]

Official publishing began in 1840, when William Colenso printed a circular to call Maori chiefs to assemble at Waitangi.[25] The government has played a large role in New Zealand, extending far beyond simply publishing government documents.[26] The largest publishing project undertaken in New Zealand was the World War II history produced by the War History Branch. The Government Printer (now GP Books) is not the only imprint. Many departments produce their own publications. The future is uncertain, since the government has announced that it should not be in the publishing business. The future mode seems to be joint publication with commercial publishers. If the *Atlas of New Zealand* is an example, they will be less comprehensive publications. The latest edition, the *Heinemann New Zealand Atlas* (1987), simply updates the physical maps of the earlier and more comprehensive publication. Publishing will continue, but is likely to be more restricted. A New Zealand collection must, nevertheless, seek to include government publications of all kinds, which will form the backbone of many subject collections, and older special series such as the *Centennial Surveys* or the *National Resources Survey* are essential for any New Zealand collection. Publications by the Ministry of the Environment, the Learning Media Group (formerly the School Publications Branch) of the Department of Education, and the Historical Publications Branch of the Department of Internal Affairs should be sought. These may become more difficult to track down in the future.

The first book with extensive New Zealand content published anywhere was John Hawkesworth's *An Account of the Voyages Undertaken by Order of His Present Majesty* ... (London: Printed for W. Strahan and

T. Cadell, 1773). This contained, among others, the report of James Cook's first voyage. There is an extensive literature on voyages of discovery in the Pacific and most of the original works are now very expensive.[27]

Accidents of time, technology, and social mores have provided more documentation concerning early New Zealand than might otherwise have been expected. The early settlers included many with literary connections in England, and Victorian society was titillated by accounts of strange places they would probably never see for themselves.[28] In general the writing is very dull, and the books fact laden, although the authenticity of those facts is now in dispute among New Zealand's current literary critics.[29] Most of these books were published in England or Australia, and were intended for a British audience.

The first novel published in New Zealand was *Taranaki,* by Major H. B. Stoney (Auckland: Wilson, 1861), a narrative of the first land war. Authors such as Samuel Butler and Lady Barker, whose works rise above the common run, were short-term settlers. F. E. Maning (pseudonym, A Pakeha Maori) produced *Old New Zealand,* which has endured. It was published in both Auckland and London in 1863, and is now the oldest New Zealand book continuously in print.

Until the 1920s most New Zealand books were published by newspapers or local printers. A. H. Reed began a press in Dunedin, which later became A. H. and A. W. Reed and moved into general publishing. It went on to become a major publisher in both Australia and New Zealand, but has become a victim of the current rage for mergers. The New Zealand business is now carried by Methuens, although there is still a Reed imprint. Its story is told in *The House of Reed* (1957) and the *House of Reed, 1957–1967* (1968). The firm of Whitcombe and Tombs (now part of Whitcoulls, a large printing and bookselling firm) published a great many New Zealand books from 1882 through the 1970s, but sold its publishing business to Penguin Books in 1988. Quality publishing in New Zealand was the hallmark of the Pegasus Press and the Caxton Press. The latter has a distinguished list to its credit and could form the basis of a special collection. Not surprisingly New Zealand's five best sellers include two cookery books and a gardening guide. Such staples sustained local publishers. Increasing interest in New Zealand has ensured, since the 1930s, a wide range of such publications. Although many of these publications were potboilers or how-to books, they provided a good financial base for their publishers.

In some ways the Oxford University Press, particularly the Clarendon imprint, functioned as a New Zealand publisher until regional publishing was devolved. This came about because of the many New Zealanders among the management and editorial staffs. It continues as a separate New Zealand publisher with a significant list of New Zealand titles. For a period the Auckland University Press was a co-publisher, and its books are still marketed overseas by Oxford.

This style of link was very common and accounts for the large number of British publisher imprints. These local houses included Penquin, Heinemann, Longmans, MacMillan, and Methuen. Among them the oldest established is Collins, which opened a New Zealand branch in 1888, but did not publish New Zealand titles regularly until the 1950s. Most, however, have now been included in Octopus Publishing Group, with several imprints.

Local publishing, i.e., by solely New Zealand houses, continues to flourish. Pauls (under various names) had a long career as a first-class publisher and continues as Longmans Paul. John McIndoe, Cape Catley, Nota Bene, and Dunmore produce books in more specialized fields. Significant also is the emergence of a feminist press, notably New Women Press, and Bridget Williams. For a period Capper Press produced fine reprints, which may still be available secondhand. Over the last twenty years the universities have become major publishers, following a period of joint publishing. The Auckland University Press, for example, has undertaken to reissue important New Zealand novels. There are many small, often fugitive, presses that fill in the gaps. These publish, among other things, a large number of poetry books.

Books are significant export and import items. Exports were valued at $34,371,753 in 1991, 0.21 percent of total exports and forty-third in rank. Most of these are for the educational market, with particular emphasis on reading kits and Pacific Island language materials, for example, the Ready to Read reading program, developed by the Ministry of Education. Exports are growing rapidly. New Zealand imported books worth $271,212,050 in 1991, 1.77 percent of all imports and eleventh in rank. Total sales internally were more than $380 million. Educational titles were preeminent and have grown some 150 percent in the last decade. At the same time, economic pressure has forced publishers to publish shorter runs and to keep titles in print for shorter times, which has meant a reduction in the numbers of titles in print. Similarly, rising local costs have resulted in an increase of actual printing overseas, which parallels the trend toward co-publishing. It is estimated that two-thirds of New Zealand books are sold to booksellers, 14 percent direct to libraries and other consumers, and the rest to retailers. These figures suffer from the same difficulties as those in the United States when trying to estimate the actual library market. Still they suggest a book economy that may be sagging but is not yet down.

Scientific and technical books are produced by a wide variety of presses, and DSIR Publishing has played a major role. The future of the latter is now somewhat uncertain.

There is a wide range of journal publishing by societies, associations, and the former DSIR agencies. Among those so active are the Polynesian Society, the New Zealand Council for Educational Research (although this may be affected by recent government decisions on funding), the New Zealand Geographical Society, the New Zealand Institute of Economic Research, the Royal Forest and Bird Protection Society, and the New Zealand Institute of International Affairs. Museums, art galleries, and libraries produce a small number of publications annually.[30] Among these are the Auckland Institute and Museum, the Auckland Public Library, the National Library of New Zealand, the Hocken Library, the Dunedin Public Library, and the National Museum of New Zealand. Although many of these publications are small, they may be the only material available on the subject, particularly in the case of exhibition catalogs.

Because New Zealand has made substantial contributions to World Literature in English, many critical works are produced in unexpected places. Selectors should be aware of the Dangaroo Press, Aarhus, Denmark; Didier, Brussels, Belgium; and watch for publications from India. There are several annual or periodic conferences on Commonwealth Literature, and most proceedings include New Zealand material. The same is true for literary and review journals.

Periodical publishing is active. Most have specific subject interests and there are few general magazines, other than popular or regional. Periodicals with a literary interest tend to be short-lived.[31] The exception is *Landfall* (Caxton Press), which has had a long and distinguished history, particularly under its first editor, Charles Brasch. The *Listener,* under a series of distinguished editors, has been a forum for reviews and short stories.

Recent trends in publishing indicate a steady output, although the proportion of fiction seems to have declined. A surprising number of books of verse continue to be published. While there may be about ten important new novels in a year, more than one thousand non-fiction titles are published. About 30–40 percent of these are educational. New Zealand appears to have adopted the anthology as the prime way of establishing a literary canon, and these anthologies are a major source for poetry and short stories. Any collection will require a substantial representation.[32]

Most literary criticism comes via the journal article and may eventually be collected. There are few major studies by individuals, although there are several of individual authors, many of which are intended for school use. One of the problems is that, in dealing with a young literature, the subjects of any criticism are still active writers, and a book, once published, goes out of date. Again, much such writing appears outside New Zealand, in such series as the Twayne International Authors. This reflects the limited internal market. For the same reason many current creative writers publish or co-publish outside New Zealand. Janet Frame, for instance, is published in the United States by Braziller, and Witi Ihimaera by Viking. It is thus difficult to avoid duplication if several approval plans are in operation.

Writers in New Zealand have to write for several markets. The local market is limited by size and location, and purely local material is unlikely to have a broad appeal. In creative writing it has caused a kind of dichotomy between those who adhere to overseas models and those who want to write in a local idiom. Since all writers want their books to sell, this has been somewhat more a matter of stance than of reality. New Zealanders have persisted in writing and have often achieved notice far beyond their native shores. Even though New Zealand literature was for many years almost a male preserve, it is instructive that those best known outside New Zealand are women: Katherine Mansfield, Janet Frame, Ngaio Marsh, Keri Hulme. Critics are now making a determined effort to recover the hidden history of women writers.[33] The same applies to Maori authors. The original retrospective national bibliography did not include many works in Maori, and most Maori writers have chosen to write in English. For most writers, until recently, success meant success abroad, and in fact most presses publish fiction only when there is the likelihood of substantial overseas sales.

Other writing, historical, economic, educational, political, or sociological, has much to offer readers from other countries. New Zealand, on the edge of the world, has had to translate others' experience into terms it could use, and to record its own experience since few others have chosen to do so. Because of the unique combination of problems faced by the nation, New Zealand studies on topics such as multi-culturalism, international relations and the role of small countries, or the economics of dependence have lessons for other countries.

The emphasis on reading has encouraged writing for children. Some of this is, of course, in the nature of school readers, but there are many stories and picture books of high quality. Margaret Mahy is probably the only author well known in the United States, but others could enrich the diversity of children's collections. The government, through the former School Publications Branch, has produced over several decades some exciting materials. This was in part because of the quality of the writing (well-known and well-acclaimed local authors were used) but also because they sought to cover awkward subjects like racial discrimination and were not afraid to rewrite accepted history. This role has been continued by the Media Learning Group, which also produces films and other non-book materials. A collection of the *School Journal*, the Secondary School Bulletins, and Correspondence School materials would be invaluable for education students and teachers.

TRADE ASSOCIATIONS

There are several associations, all listed with their officers in *New Zealand Books in Print (NZBIP)*. The following list provides only the names and addresses.

Book Publishers Association of New Zealand, Inc.
    94 Newton Road   or P.O. Box 44-146
    Newton   Point Chevalier
    Auckland 3   Auckland 2

Copyright Licensing, Ltd.
    (address as above)

Booksellers Association of New Zealand
    Book House   or P.O. Box 11377
    86 Boulcott Street   Wellington
    Wellington

Book Marketing Council
    (address as above)

Copyright Council of New Zealand, Inc.
    P.O. Box 8028
    Wellington

Queen Elizabeth II Arts Council of New Zealand
    The Manager, Literature Program
    P.O. Box 3806
    Wellington

NEW ZEALAND LITERARY AWARDS

A full listing, with officers, addresses, and lists of recent recipients appears in *New Zealand Books in Print.* Only the names and brief descriptions are given here.

New Zealand Book Awards (for poetry, fiction, and non-fiction)
AIM Children's Book Awards
Goodman Fielder Wattie Book Award (3 annually)
Choysa Awards for Children's Illustrators
New Zealand Library Association Book Award (children's non-fiction)
    Esther Glenn Award (children's fiction)
    Russell Clark Award (children's illustrator)
PEN (New Zealand Centre) Best First Book Awards
    Best First Book of Prose Award (incorporating the Hubert Church Award)
    Best First Book of Poetry Award (incorporating the Jessie McKay Award)
Reed Fiction Award (in association with the *Listener*)
Sunday Star and Whitcoulls Short Story Competition
Talking Book of the Year Awards

ASSISTANCE TO WRITERS

Queen Elizabeth II Arts Council. Literary Program
  Scholarship in Letters
  Writing Bursary
  Major Project Grants
  Non-fiction Assistance Fund
  Non-fiction Grants to Writers
  Discretionary Grants
  Overseas Travel Bursary
  Overseas Travel Assistance
  Award for Achievement
Katherine Mansfield Memorial Fellowship
Louis Johnson New Writers' Bursary
Playwrights Award
Frank Sargeson Trust
Auckland University Writers' Fellowship
Canterbury University Writers' Fellowship
Robert Burns Fellowship (Otago University)
Victoria University Writers' Fellowship
Waikato University Writers' Fellowship

CONFERENCES

Association for Commonwealth Literature and Language Studies (European Branch) ACLALS
Commonwealth Institute (London) Working Party on Library Resources
New Zealand Library Association. Annual Conference, and others for kinds of libraries or special topics
South Pacific Association for Commonwealth Literature and Language Studies (SPACLALS)

These conferences sometimes produce proceedings, but mostly papers are printed in periodicals or are published separately.

Selection and Acquisition

CURRENT IMPRINTS

General information concerning current imprints is available from several sources. The most complete are the *New Zealand National Bibliography* (microfiche and online) and *New Zealand Books in Print*. The *Journal of Commonwealth Literature* contains an annual bibliography, which covers non-fiction as well as literature. The *MLA International Bibliography* includes books and articles of criticism from all countries, but does not cover original writing. *Pacific Studies* includes a list of Selected Acquisitions in the various Hawaiian libraries. Because of small print runs, titles listed in such sources may be unobtainable. Similarly, reviews and review articles that may be the only critical references to poetry or other fugitive works often appear long after publication. Reviews and critical essays are widely dispersed. The only local approach to a general reviewing periodical is *New Zealand Books*.

Because much writing about New Zealand appears in other countries, general and topical reviews must be scanned. If the library has approval plans for U.S. and U.K. publications, books received should be reviewed to determine whether they include New Zealand-related titles. Series such as those produced by the Hakluyt Society also contain volumes relating to New Zealand.

A range of dealers will be necessary. Some offer approval or blanket order plans. These include: James Bennett, New Zealand Export Books, and South Pacific Books. Bennett's University Book Centre, Palmerston North, New Zealand, can fulfill direct orders. The same is probably still true of Roy Parsons Bookseller, Lambton Quay, Wellington, New Zealand, and Hyndmans Booksellers, Dunedin, New Zealand, but few are set up to seek and supply the range of books appropriate to a New Zealand collection.

For New Zealand government publications the best way is through GP Publications, Ltd., P.O. Box 38-900, Petone, Wellington, New Zealand, but complete coverage is difficult to obtain. Lawrence Verry has been the U.S. agent for government publications for some years.

While Auckland University Press publications are available through the Oxford University Press, other university presses will supply direct. Otago University Press has a marketing arrangement with John McIndoe, another New Zealand publisher.

Other publishers often have U.S. representatives or agencies or co-publishing agreements for some titles. Be aware, however, that publishers with regional or national affiliates do not always have established arrangements for handling their imprints.

Periodicals can be obtained through Hills Library and Information Service, Private Bag, Newmarket, Auckland, New Zealand, although legal serials usually have to be obtained from the publishers.

RETROSPECTIVE SELECTION

The primary bibliographic source is Bagnall, but many of the works cited in this essay will provide beginning or rounding-out lists. The changes in New Zealand publishing, mentioned earlier, can make it very difficult to track down recent books whose listed publisher is no longer in business, or titles which have been sold to another publisher, and now bear a new imprint. Older bibliographic aids can be misleading in such conditions.

Although *NZBIP* lists a surprising number of older titles, the vast majority are out of print. Since many of these were widely distributed, and are joined by the many titles that were first published outside New Zealand, searching for them can be time-consuming. There are two partial guides that can help: (1) Barry Fisher, *Guide to New Zealand Book Collecting* (Dunedin: City Publishers, 1977) (although idiosyncratic in approach, and mostly given to estimating prices for individual books, which will, of course, now be out of date, it can nevertheless provide some leads); and (2) Brian R. Howes, *Guide to Fine and Rare Australasian Books* (Wagga Wagga, NSW: the Author, 1986). Despite its title it does include some New Zealand materials. One of the major sources for older New Zealand material is the annual auction by J. H. Bethune and Co., Ltd., P.O. Box 63, Wellington, New Zealand. Libraries can ask for the auction catalog and send in bids, or ask a local librarian to bid for them. The prices used to be listed in a guide by Andrew Fair, but this has not been published since 1975.

Other New Zealand secondhand dealers are listed in *NZBIP,* and a select list is provided in appendix D. Specialties are suggested in the *NZBIP* listing and should be checked against library interests.

The Cook Bicentenary, the Australian Bicentenary, and New Zealand's Sesquicentenary have had effects both on the prices and the availability of antiquarian materials, especially those relating to early discovery and exploration. Adam Matthews Publications, 8 Oxford St., Marlborough, Wiltshire, SN8 1AP, England, are in the course of producing a microfilm project on the history of science and technology. Series Two: *The Papers of Sir Joseph Banks, 1743–1820,* includes significant material relating to the discovery of New Zealand. Occasional reprints become available. The same is true for books of natural history, many of which have outstanding illustrations. Nevertheless titles can be found from widely scattered dealers throughout the world. Some are listed in appendix D.

ARCHIVES AND U.S. LIBRARY COLLECTIONS

Archival materials of their nature are not usually for sale. Libraries should, however, be aware of what is available. The Colonial Office papers, including several series concerning New Zealand, were published in reprint by Mansell. Many series have been microfilmed by the National Libraries of Australia and New Zealand, and the Genealogical Library Collections in Salt Lake City should not be overlooked. Readex, 59 Pine St., New Canaan, CT 06840-5426, and Adam Matthews Publications provide many microfilm and microfiche editions of British official papers. Publications by Mander-Jones and others can be used to direct researchers to the appropriate libraries.

There are several U.S. libraries with outstanding New Zealand collections. Among them are Yale University, Penn State (University Park), UCLA, UC San Diego, and University of Texas, Austin. Only Penn State has produced a catalog, but online access is possible to most of the other collections. I. R. Willison provides a history of collection development at the British Library, which contains useful comments and hints on collecting in support of Australian and New Zealand studies.[34] Other U.K. sources are listed by Valerie Bloomfield in the report listed under "Other Bibliographies" in appendix B.

Conclusion

While the study of New Zealand is still not widespread as an academic topic, there is wider interest in its literature and history. An area studies collection will pay attention to the academic interests of the institution. Specialized libraries will need to have materials in their own fields. Public libraries on the Pacific coast will find increasing interest in the lands down under, and New Zealand with its large Maori population and its commitment to non-nuclear status provides a vocal example of the small country's point of view in this world. Even without the intention of creating a New Zealand collection, selected titles from its fiction and non-fiction can enrich any collection as, for example, books about the *Greenpeace* incident and the French nuclear tests in the Pacific, or children's stories about the Maori, or the world-acclaimed novels of its best authors. Travel to the South Pacific has become very popular, and collections should include more than the regular guidebooks produced in series. The ecological lessons that can be learned from New Zealand are important to other countries, and its history provides outstanding examples, both good and bad. New Zealand has produced outstanding people in many walks of life, for example, Sir Ernest Rutherford, who first split the atom, or Sir Robert Cotton, an important geomorphologist, Arthur Lydiard, the international Olympic coach, Sir Edmund Hillary, who first climbed Mount Everest, Dame Kiri Te Kanawha and Inia Te Waiata, of operatic fame, and New Zealanders themselves have been New Zealand's principal export. A New Zealand collection can help show how they have contributed to the world and to down under. For such reasons there is a place for New Zealand books in all types of libraries. Collecting them may not always be easy, but there is a good bibliographic and commercial support structure.

Appendix A. Guides to New Zealand

First listed are general guides. These are followed by studies of particular subjects. Some may well be out of print. When known, this is so indicated.

GENERAL GUIDES

Bloomfield, G. T. *New Zealand: A Handbook of Historical Statistics.* Boston: G. K. Hall, 1984. ISBN 0816181683

Dictionary of New Zealand Biography. v. 1– . 1990– . Wellington: GP Books and various co-publishers, 1990– . It will be issued in 5–6 volumes, and a Maori version, entitled *Nga Tangata Taumata Rau,* is under way.

Dictionary of New Zealand Biography. Ed. G. H. Scholefield. 2 vols. Wellington: Department of Internal Affairs, 1940. o/p. Still useful but dated both in content and approach.

Encyclopedia of New Zealand. Ed. A. H. McLintock. 3 vols. Wellington: Government Printer, 1966. o/p. Although dated, this is still the most complete encyclopedia and should be part of any New Zealand collection.

Heinemann New Zealand Dictionary. Ed. H. W. Orsman. Auckland: Heinemann, 1979. Current edition (1989) by Octopus Group Publishers. ISBN 0790000164

Historical Records of New Zealand. Ed. Robert McNab. 2 vols. Wellington: Government Printer, 1908–14. A facsimile reprint was issued in 1973.

Illustrated Encyclopedia of New Zealand. Ed. Gordon McLauchlan. Auckland: David Bateman, 1986. ISBN 186930071. This has some errors and omissions, but provides newer material not found in McLintock.

Monthly Abstract of Statistics. v. 1– . Wellington: Department of Statistics, 1947– .

New Zealand Atlas. Ed. Ian Wards. Wellington: Government Printer, 1976. ISBN 0477010008. Now out of print, but still the best atlas. An earlier edition edited by A. H. McLintock is now a collector's item.

New Zealand Official Yearbook. Wellington: Department of Statistics 1892– . Each issue contains special articles and a bibliography.

Reed. A. W. *Place Names in New Zealand.* Wellington: Reed, 1975. (Supplement, 1979)

Who's Who in New Zealand. Auckland: Reed, 1991 (latest ed.). ISBN 0790002248

Wise's New Zealand Guide: A Gazetteer of New Zealand. 7th ed. Ed. John A. Cullen. Auckland: Wise's Publications, 1979.

TOPICAL

Beaglehole, John Cawte. *The Exploration of New Zealand.* London: Adam and Charles Black, 1966.

Docking, Gil. *Two Hundred Years of New Zealand Painting.* Rev. ed. Auckland: Bateman, 1990. ISBN 1869530454

Evans, Patrick. *The Penguin History of New Zealand Literature*. Auckland: Penguin, 1990. ISBN 0140113711. More idiosyncratic than the *Oxford History*, but a valuable balance.

New Zealand: Pacific Land Down Under. Ed. Kenneth B. Cumberland. Wellington: Reed, 1973. ISBN 0589007734. Although in appearance a coffee-table book, this is the best geographical study of the country.

Oxford History of New Zealand. Ed. W. H. Oliver. Auckland: Oxford University Press, 1987. ISBN 019558063X

Oxford History of New Zealand Literature in English. Ed. Terry Sturm. Auckland: Oxford University Press, 1991. ISBN 019558211X. This book contains a useful summary of New Zealand publishing and an updated bibliography by John Thompson.

Oxford Illustrated History of New Zealand. Ed. Keith Sinclair. Auckland: Oxford University Press, 1990. ISBN 0195582098

Shaw, Peter, and Robin Morrison. *New Zealand Architecture: From Polynesian Beginnings to 1990*. Auckland: Hodder & Stoughton, 1991. ISBN 034053320X

Sinclair, Keith. *A History of New Zealand*. Rev. ed. Auckland: Penguin, 1988. ISBN 0140228217

Thomson, John Mansfield. *The Oxford History of New Zealand Music*. Auckland: Oxford University Press, 1991. ISBN 0195581768. Uneven coverage, but the only general survey available.

MAORITANGA

The following books suggest some of the kinds of materials available, but there are no recent comprehensive books.

Barlow, Clive. *Tikanga Whakaara: Key Concepts in Maori Culture*. Auckland: Oxford University Press, 1991. ISBN 0195582128

Best, Eldon. *The Maori*. Wellington: Board of Maori Ethnological Research for the Author and the Polynesian Society, 1929. 2 vols. (Reprinted 1941) Polynesian Society Memoir, no. 5. Out of date in some respects but still the single most comprehensive study.

Biggs, Bruce. *Complete English-Maori Dictionary*. Auckland: Auckland University Press, Oxford University Press, 1981. ISBN 0196479894

―――― *English-Maori Maori-English Dictionary*. Auckland: Auckland University Press, 1991. ISBN 0869499577

Hiroa, Te Rangi (Peter Buck). *The Coming of the Maori*. Wellington: Maori Purposes Fund Board and Whitcombe and Tombs, 1924. (Reprint of 2nd ed., 1950) o/p

Metge, Joan. *The Maori of New Zealand: Rautahi*. 2nd ed. London: Routledge & Kegan Paul, 1976.

Pool, Ian. *Te Iwi Maori: Population Past, Present and Projected*. Auckland: Auckland University Press, 1990. ISBN 1869400496

Ryan, P. M. *A Dictionary of Modern Maori*. Rev. ed. Auckland: Octopus Publishing Group, 1989. ISBN 0868356685

Smith, S. Percy. *History and Traditions of the Maoris of the West Coast of North Island, New Zealand Prior to 1840.* Auckland: Pukapuka, 1991. A classic originally published in 1910 in a limited edition of three hundred copies.
Te Ao Hurihuri: The World Moves On. Ed. Michael King. Rev. ed. Auckland: Reed, 1992. ISBN 0790002396
Tihe Mauri Ora: Aspects of Maoritanga. Ed. Michael King. Wellington: Methuen New Zealand, 1978. ISBN 088635685
Vasil, Raj. *Biculturalism: Reconciling Aotearoa with New Zealand.* Wellington: Victoria University Press, 1989. ISBN 0864731655
Williams, Herbert W. *A Dictionary of the Maori Language.* 7th ed., rev. and enl. Wellington: GPO, 1979. (Latest printing 1985) ISBN 0477012957. Updated version of the first Maori dictionary.

Appendix B. Guides to the Literature

There are numerous books that provide an overview of specific subjects up to the time they were published, but only a few that can supply current information. Nor are there exact equivalents of the *Publishers Weekly* or the *Times Literary Supplement,* the closest being *New Zealand Books.* The following entries set out some of the materials available, without any pretense that they provide complete coverage. The bibliographic entries that follow them give wider coverage, but, not having annotations, do not provide a full sense of the contents.

SURVEYS

Jones, Joseph, and Johanna Jones. *New Zealand Fiction.* Boston: Twayne, 1984. The first extensive survey published outside New Zealand.
Journal of Commonwealth Literature has a survey of literature in the second issue each year, together with a comprehensive bibliography.
Martin, Murray, S. "Writing Down Under: Recent Literature from Australia, New Zealand and the Pacific Islands," *Choice* 14, no. 1 (1977): 19–31.
——— "New Zealand at 150: A Sesquicentennial Booklist," *Choice* 27, no. 4 (1990): 1460–64.
Reid, John Cowie. *New Zealand Non-fiction: A Survey with Notes.* Wellington: Price-Milburn, 1968.
Stevens, Joan. *The New Zealand Novel, 1860–1965.* 2nd ed. Wellington: Reed, 1966.
Three Hundred Years of New Zealand Books: Being a Select Chronological Listing and Commentary, Primarily But Not Solely Literary, from Tasman to 1975. Comp. Peter Alcock and William Broughton. Palmerston North: English Department, Massey University, 1986.

BIBLIOGRAPHIES

The national bibliography has developed in a somewhat oblique fashion, with many participants, and much backing and filling. From the start there has been confusion about recording and including Maori publications. A short history of the project by A. G. Bagnall sets out general purposes and problems.[35] For such reasons the first entries provide a chronological history of its development. They are followed by other supplementary bibliographical entries.

THE NATIONAL BIBLIOGRAPHY

Thompson, Arthur S. *The Story of New Zealand: Past and Present.* London: Eyre & Spottiswoode, 1859. (Reprint, New York: Praeger, 1970) Bibliography, v. 2, pp. 341–62.

Collier, James. *The Literature Relating to New Zealand: A Bibliography.* Wellington: Government Printer, 1889.

A Bibliography of the Literature Relating to New Zealand. Ed. T. M. Hocken. Wellington: Government Printer, 1909. (Reprint, Wellington: Newrick Associates, 1973) Cited as *Hocken.*

Johnstone, A. H. *Supplement to Hocken's Bibliography of New Zealand Literature.* Christchurch: Whitcombe & Tombs, 1927. (Reprinted 1975)

Chapple, L. J. B. *A Bibliographical Brochure Containing Addenda and Corrigenda to Extant Bibliographies of New Zealand Literature.* Wellington: Reed, 1938. Cited as *Chapple.*

Index to New Zealand Periodicals and Current National Bibliography. 1950–65. Wellington: National Library Service, 1951–66.

New Zealand National Bibliography to the Year 1960. Ed. Austin Graham Bagnall. 5 vols. Wellington: Government Printer, 1969–75. Cited as *Bagnall.*

New Zealand National Bibliography. 1966–85.Wellington: National Library of New Zealand, 1968–86. The following years are available on microfiche, and also online. There is a monthly printed list, but it is not cumulative and has no index.

Index to New Zealand Periodicals, 1968–86. Now superseded by *Index New Zealand,* 1987– and incorporated into KIWINET.

A number of complementary and supplementary works are available:

A Bibliography of New Zealand Bibliographies. Wellington: New Zealand Library Association, 1967. A combination of previous annual lists. Now maintained online by the Waikato University Library.

Harvey, D. R. *Union List of New Zealand Newspapers before 1940 Preserved in Libraries, Newspaper Offices, Local Authority Offices, and Museums in New Zealand.* Wellington: National Library of New Zealand, 1985 (paper and microfiche). ISBN 0477060447. Maori ed., ISBN 0477060455.

Norman, Philip. *Bibliography of New Zealand Compositions.* 3rd ed. Christchurch: Nota Bene Music Publishing Cooperative, 1991. ISBN 1869350510

Rodger, Margaret D. *Theses on the History of New Zealand.* 4 vols. Palmerston North: Massey University, 1968–72.

Union List of Theses of the University of New Zealand, 1910–1954. Wellington: New Zealand Library Association, 1956. Supplements cover 1955–75.

Williams, H. W. *A Bibliography of Printed Maori to 1900, and Supplement.* Wellington: Government Printer, 1975.

OTHER BIBLIOGRAPHIES

Albinski, Nan. *Australian/New Zealand Literature in the Pennsylvania State University Libraries.* University Park, Pa.: The Library, 1989. An annotated catalog of one of the larger American collections.

Bloomfield, Valerie. *Resources for Australian and New Zealand Studies; A Guide to Library Holdings in the United Kingdom.* London: Sir Robert Menzies Centre for Australian Studies and the British Library, 1988.

Burns, James. *New Zealand Novels and Novelists, 1861–1979: An Annotated Bibliography.* Auckland: Heinemann, 1981. ISBN 0868633720

Dornbusch, C. E. *The New Zealand Army; A Bibliography.* Cornwallville, N.Y.: Hope Farm Press, 1961.

Griffiths, D. J. *Books of Southern New Zealand Listed by Locality.* Dunedin: Otago Heritage Board, 1989. ISBN 0908774060

Grover, Ray. *New Zealand.* Oxford; Santa Barbara: Clio, 1980. (World Bibliographic Series, vol. 18) ISBN 0903450313

Guide to New Zealand Information Sources. Part 1– . Palmerston North: Massey University Press, 1975– .
Pt. 1. Plants and Animals, by L. E. Battye, 1975.
Pt. 2A. Farming, Field and Horticultural Crops, by N. Thompson, 1977.
Pt. 2B. Livestock Farming, Fisheries and Forestry, by C. R. Cherrie, 1979.
Pt. 3. Education, by L. E. Battye, 1977.
Pt. 4. Religion, by L. E. Marsden, 1980.
Pt. 5. Official Publications, by C. L. Carpenter, 1980.
Pt. 6. History, by V. J. Hector, 1982.

Harvey, Douglas Ross. *Bibliography of Writings about New Zealand Music Published to the End of 1983.* Wellington: Victoria University Press, 1985. ISBN 0864730292

——— *Music at National Archives: Sources for the Study of Music in New Zealand.* Christchurch: Canterbury University School of Music, 1991. ISBN 0908718020

Mander-Jones, Phyllis. *Manuscripts in the British Isles Relating to Australia and New Zealand.* Honolulu: University of Hawaii Press, 1972. ISBN 0824802047

New Zealand Books in Print. 1979– . Melbourne: D. W. Thorpe, 1979– . Contains other information relating to publishing; does not cover all government publications.

Sargison, Patricia A. *Victoria's Farthest Daughters: A Bibliography of Published Sources for the Study of Women in New Zealand, 1830–1914.* Wellington: Alexander Turnbull Library Endowment Trust with the New Zealand Founders Society, 1984. ISBN 0908702019

Smyth, Bernard W., and Hillary Howorth. *Books and Pamphlets Relating to Culture and the Arts in New Zealand: A Bibliography Including Works Published to the End of the Year 1977.* Christchurch: Department of Extension Studies, University of Canterbury; Wellington: New Zealand Commission for UNESCO, Department of Internal Affairs, 1978.

Taylor, C. R. H. *A Bibliography of Publications on the New Zealand Maori and the Moriori of the Chatham Islands.* Oxford: Clarendon Press, 1972.

—— *A Pacific Bibliography: Printed Matter Relating to the Native Peoples of Polynesia, Melanesia, and Micronesia.* 2nd ed. Oxford: Clarendon Press, 1965. Sections II A and II H are of particular relevance to New Zealand.

Thompson, John. *New Zealand Literature to 1977: A Guide to Information Sources.* Detroit: Gale, 1980. ISBN 0810312468. The author states that his bibliography in *The Oxford History of New Zealand Literature* extends and replaces this work, but the notes and annotations are more complete here for the period covered.

Traue, J. E. *New Zealand Studies: Guide to the Bibliographic Resources.* Wellington: Victoria University Press, 1985. ISBN 0684730330

Turner, Harold W. *Bibliography of New Religious Movements in Primal Societies.* v. 3: *Oceania.* Boston: G. K. Hall, 1990. ISBN 0816189846. Volume 3 contains a considerable amount of material on the Maori missions, and on local cults and religions.

Wood, G. A. *Studying New Zealand History.* 2nd ed., rev. by Simon Cauchi and G. A. Wood. Dunedin: University of Otago Press, 1992. A scholarly approach to the use of local and overseas resources.

Appendix C. Review Sources

Archifacts: Bulletin of the Archives and Records Association of New Zealand. Wellington: The Association, 1977– . Irregular.

Australian and New Zealand Studies in Canada. v. 1– . 1989– . London, Ontario: Department of English, University of Western Ontario. Biannual.

Climate; A Journal of New Zealand and Australian Writing. v. 1– . 1959– . Biannual.

Comment. n.s. v. 1– . 1977– . Quarterly.

Forest and Bird. v. 1– . 1923– . Wellington: Royal Forest and Bird Protection Society. Quarterly.

Journal of New Zealand Literature. v. 1– . 1983– . Sponsored in turn by University Departments of English. Annual. Currently, Department of English, University of Otago, Dunedin.

Journal of the Polynesian Society. v. 1– . 1892– . Wellington: The Society. Quarterly.

Journal of the Royal Society of New Zealand. v. 1– . 1971– . Wellington: The Society. Quarterly. First published in 1868 as *Transactions of the New Zealand Institute,* it is the country's oldest periodical

Landfall: A New Zealand Quarterly. v. 1– . 1947– . Christchurch: Caxton Press. Quarterly. The only long-lasting periodical devoted to literature and the arts in New Zealand.

Listener. 1939– . Wellington: Broadcasting Council of New Zealand. Weekly. Also titled *New Zealand Listener,* and usually so cited. It contains reviews and original writing.

New Zealand Books. v. 1– . 1991– . Quarterly. Reviews and feature articles. J. M. Thompson, Peppercorn Press, P.O. Box 28-063, Kelburn, Wellington.

New Zealand Economic Papers. v. 1– . 1966– . Wellington: New Zealand Association of Economists. Annual.

New Zealand Geographer. v. 1– . 1945– . Christchurch: New Zealand Geographic Society. Biannual.

New Zealand Journal of History. v. 1– . 1967– . Auckland: Department of History, University of Auckland. Biannual.

New Zealand Libraries. v. 1– . 1937– . Wellington: The New Zealand Library Association. Bimonthly. Carries reviews, commentary, and other informative articles.

New Zealand Monthly Review. v. 1– . 1960– . Christchurch: The New Zealand Monthly Review Society.

Pacific Studies: A Journal Devoted to the Study of the Pacific—Its Islands and the Adjacent Countries. v. 1– . 1978– . Laie, Hawaii: Institute for Pacific Studies. Quarterly. This journal contains reviews and lists of publications received by several Hawaiian libraries.

Pacific Viewpoint. v. 1– . 1960– . Wellington: Department of Geography, Victoria University of Wellington. Biannual.

Political Science. v. 1– . 1948– . Wellington: School of Political Science and Public Affairs, Victoria University of Wellington. Biannual.

Turnbull Library Record. v. 1– . 1946– . Wellington: Friends of the Turnbull Library. Biannual. Also contains lists of important accessions.

University of Hawaii Pacific Collection. *Acquisitions List.* Honolulu. Quarterly.

Sporadic reviews appear in many general and literary periodicals, including *Times Literary Supplement, New York Times Book Review, Choice,* and *World Literature Today.* The *MLA International Bibliography* includes citations for books as well as journals.

Appendix D. Book Dealers

James Bennett, Collaroy, NSW
U.S. address:
P.O. Box 3617
Daly City, CA 94015
   They will provide individual books or support collecting plans.

New Zealand Export Books
P.O. Box 14054
Hamilton, New Zealand
   They provide a bimonthly list of significant new publications, which now include some Australian publications. Series standing orders and blanket orders or profiles are handled. They will provide government and society publications. Specialties are literature, history, education, and the sciences.

South Pacific Books
P.O. Box 3533
Auckland, New Zealand
   They supply selection slips for New Zealand, Australian, and South Pacific publications, and will search for other titles.

ANTIQUARIAN DEALERS

Messrs. Berkelouw
P.O. Box 41
Rushcutters Bay
NSW 2011, Australia
   General materials on Australia and New Zealand, especially literature and travel.

Cellar Bookshop
  18090 Wyoming
  Detroit, MI 48221
    General interest in the Pacific.

Dawsons of Pall Mall
  16 and 17 Pall Mall
  London SW1Y 5NB, United Kingdom
    Particularly good for travel.

Dreamers Bookshop
  112 Rimu Road
  Paraparaumu, New Zealand
    Maori and art books.

Anah Dunsheath
  6 High Street
  Auckland 1, New Zealand
    Early and rare books, New
  Zealand, and Pacific.

Marlborough Rare Books Ltd.
  35 Old Bond Street
  London W1X 4PT, United Kingdom
    Travel and natural history.

Oriental Book Store
  630 East Colorado Boulevard
  Pasadena, CA 91030
    Asian and Pacific materials.

Parmer Books
  7644 Forrestal Road
  San Diego, CA 92120-2203
    Voyages and travel.

Bernard Quaritch
  5-8 Lower John Street
  Golden Square
  London W1R 4AV, United Kingdom
    General Pacific, rare books.

Quilter's Bookshop
  110 Lambton Quay
  (P.O Box 958)
  Wellington, New Zealand
    General New Zealand, not so
  much literature.

Gaston Renard
  G.P.O. Box 5235BB
  Melbourne, Victoria 3181, Australia
    Literature.

Smith's Bookshop
  133 Manchester Street
  Christchurch 1, New Zealand
    Maori culture, literature.

Smith's Bookshop-Rowan Gibbs
  P.O. Box 10-265
  Wellington, New Zealand
    New Zealand and Pacific
  literature.

Henry Sotheran Ltd.
  2,3,4 and 5 Sackville St. Piccadilly
  London W1X 2DP, United Kingdom
    Natural history and fine printing.

Stratford Books
  223 Dominion Road
  (P.O. Box 26-150)
  Mount Eden
  Auckland, New Zealand
    New Zealand and Pacific books.

Terrace Bookshop
  223 Stuart Street
  Dunedin, New Zealand
    Art, New Zealand, music scores,
  and sheet music.

Tusitala Bookshop
  116 Hekili Street
  Kailua, HI 96734

Notes

1. Raewyn Dalziel, "Patterns of Settlement," in *New Zealand Atlas,* ed. Ian Wards (Wellington: Government Printer, 1976), pp. 53–56; and David McGill, *The Other New Zealanders* (Wellington: Mallinson Rendel, 1982), which deals with the other 20 percent who are neither of British nor of Maori descent.
2. The classic work is *Tutira: The Story of a New Zealand Sheep Station,* by H. Guthrie Smith, 4th. ed. (Wellington: Reed, 1969). Other useful books are: Andrew Hill Clark, *The Invasion of New Zealand by Plants and Animals: The South Island* (Westport, Conn.: Greenwood, 1970); L. V. McCaskill,

Hold This Land: A History of Soil Conservation in New Zealand (Wellington: Reed, 1973), ISBN 0589007084; A. Grenfell Price, *The Western Invasion of the Pacific and Its Continents: A Study of Merging Frontiers and Changing Landscapes, 1513–1958* (Oxford: Clarendon, 1963); Graham Searle, *Rush to Destruction: An Appraisal of the New Zealand Beech Forest Controversy* (Wellington: Reed, 1975); and *Society and the Environment in New Zealand*, ed. R. J. Johnston (Christchurch: Whitcombe and Tombs for the New Zealand Geographic Society, 1974), ISBN 0723304033. These books also contain numerous references. A more wide-ranging book with New Zealand references is *Ecological Imperialism: The Biological Expansion of Europe, 900–1900*, by Alfred W. Crosby (Cambridge: Cambridge University Press, 1986), ISBN 0521220097.

3. Although somewhat dated, *National Parks of New Zealand*, ed. John Pascoe, 3rd ed. (Wellington: Government Printer, 1974) offers a good overview of the diversity within the park system. A later publication, now also out of print, is *The Fold of the Land: New Zealand's National Parks from the Air*, by Lloyd Homer and Les Molloy (Wellington: Allen and Unwin, 1988), an example of joint public-private publishing.

4. Some idea of the problems behind the recovery of Maori traditions and myths can be gained from the following articles: Judith Binney, "Maori Oral Narrations, Pakeha Written Texts: Two Forms of Telling History," *New Zealand Journal of History* 20, no. 1 (1987): 16–28; Ruth Brown, "Maori Spirituality as a Pakeha Construct," *Meanjin* 48, no. 2 (1989): 252–58; Margaret Orbell, "The Religious Significance of Maori Migration Traditions," *Journal of the Polynesian Society* 84, no. 3 (1990): 1460–64. The principal text on Polynesian voyaging is: C. A. Sharp, *Ancient Voyages in Polynesia*, 2nd ed. (Hamilton: Paul's Book Arcade; Berkeley: University of California Press, 1963–64.) These views have been disputed, and a contrary opinion can be found in David Lewis *From Maui to Cook: The Discovery and Settlement of the Pacific* (Sydney: Doubleday, 1977), ISBN 086824001X. The myths themselves have been under scrutiny; see David R. Simmons, *The Great New Zealand Myth: A Study of the Discovery and Origin Tradition of the Maori* (Wellington: Reed, 1976).

5. For an account of James Cook's experiences in New Zealand, see *James Cook and New Zealand* by A. Charles Begg and Neil C. Begg (Wellington: Government Printer, 1969).

6. A good general survey can be found in Ernest S. Dodge, *New England and the South Seas* (Cambridge, Mass.: Harvard University Press, 1965).

7. Peter Adams. *Fatal Necessity: British Intervention in New Zealand, 1830–1847* (Auckland: Auckland University Press; Wellington, London: Oxford University Press, 1977).

8. Edward Gibbon Wakefield in *A Letter from Sydney* (1829) outlined his principles for colonization, and, later, he and his brothers put them into practice in New Zealand.

9. A wide-ranging review of the treaty and its results can be found in: *Waitangi: Maori and Pakeha Perspectives of the Treaty of Waitangi*, ed K. H. Kawharu (Auckland: Oxford University Press, 1989), ISBN 019558175X.

10. Opposing views can be found in: C. K. Stead, "Keri Hulme's *'the bone people,'* and the Pegasus Award for Maori Literature," *Ariel* 16 (1985): 101–8, and Margery Fee, "Why C. K. Stead Didn't Like Keri Hulme's *the bone people:* Who Can Write as Other?" *Australian and New Zealand Studies in Canada,* no. 1 (1989): 11–32. (This article contains an extensive bibliography.)

11. Sharon Dell, "The Maori Book or the Book in Maori," *New Zealand Libraries* 45, no. 5 (1987): 98–101; Jane McRae, "The Maori People and Libraries, *NZL* 46, no. 1 (1990): 8–12; and Lyn Williams, "Adopting a Bicultural Stance over Reference Services in New Zealand Libraries," *NZL* 46, no. 11 (1991): 21–25. A fuller examination of bi-culturalism in education can be found in *Polynesian and Pakeha in New Zealand Education,* ed. Douglas Bray and Clement Hill, 2 vols. (Auckland: Heinemann Educational, 1973), ISBN 0868632716.

12. The "Old Dominions" are Australia, Canada, and New Zealand, and, formerly, South Africa.

13. Geoffrey Palmer, *Unbridled Power? An Interpretation of New Zealand's Constitution and Government* (Wellington: Oxford University Press, 1979), ISBN 0195581709, and Richard Mulgan, *Democracy and Power in New Zealand: A Study of New Zealand Politics,* 2nd ed. (Auckland: Oxford University Press, 1989), ISBN 0125582004.

14. A useful survey of politics can be found in *Electoral Behaviour in New Zealand,* ed. Martin Holland (Auckland: Oxford University Press, 1992), ISBN 0195582616. It contains good, select bibliography.

15. An early example is the leadership of Peter Fraser in attempting to forestall the Great Power veto in the United Nations, when that institution was being formed in 1946.

16. *Culture and Identity in New Zealand,* eds. David Novitz and Bill Willmott (Wellington: GP Books, 1989) presents a series of essays that suggest how the current sense of New Zealand identity was achieved.

17. An article in *Newsweek* 98, no. 3 (Dec 2, 1991): 51–53, places New Zealand first in the world for teaching reading.

18. Helen B. Cowey, "National Library Extension Division: Background Notes," *NZL* 46, no. 1 (1974): 69–79; Liz McLean, "From Review to Reform. The 1987 Review of National Library Services to Rural Areas in the Context of the 1989 Local Government Reform," *NZL* 46, no. 4 (1990): 24–27; Peter Scott, "The National Library's Roles in a Changing Environment," *NZL* 46, no. 1 (1991): 2–4, and "Change to National Library's Services to Public Libraries," *Library Life,* no. 151 (Sept., 1991): 1.

19. Maxine K. Rochester, *The Revolution in New Zealand Librarianship* (Halifax, N.S.: Dalhousie University, School of Library and Information Studies, 1990).

20. W. J. McEldowney, *New Zealand University Library Resources, 1982* (Dunedin: University of Otago Library for the Committee of New Zealand University Librarians, 1983).

21. David M. Taylor's *The Oldest Manuscripts in New Zealand* (Wellington: New Zealand Council for Educational Research, 1955) gives some idea of the

range and diversity of holdings in all types of libraries. Although superseded by the register maintained by the Turnbull Library, it contains full descriptions of all manuscripts.

22. Gwen Gawaith, "New Zealand," in *School Libraries: International Developments,* ed. Jean E. Lowrie and Mieko Nagakura, 2nd ed. (Metuchen, N.J.: Scarecrow, 1991), pp. 313–21.

23. Monica Hissink, "CRI-ing: 'From DNA to the Dinner Plate'; Science Restructuring Implications for Government Research Libraries and . . . University Libraries?" *NZL* 46, no. 11 (1991): 5–9.

24. An excellent survey is provided by Dennis McEldowney in "Publishing, Patronage, Literary Magazines," in *The Oxford History of New Zealand Literature in English,* ed. Terry Sturm (Auckland: Oxford University Press, 1990), pp. 545–600, and a history of printing can be found in: *150 Years of New Zealand Printing,* ed. Tolla Willament (Wellington: Government Printing Office, 1985).

25. W. A. Glue, *History of the Government Printing Office* (Wellington: Government Printer, 1966).

26. A useful historical survey is provided by Pleasance Purser, "Production, Distribution and Bibliographic Control of New Zealand Government Publications," *NZL* 45, no. 12 (1988): 286–89.

27. The Hill Collection of Pacific Voyages in the Library of the University of California, San Diego, is one of the best in the United States, and a three-volume bibliography was published by the library in 1974–83. Recent antiquarian catalogs, for example, indicate that the original editions of Cook's *Journals* may sell for as much as $17,000. Where reprints or scholarly editions are available, these can be substituted. The Hakluyt Society publication series include many New Zealand- and Pacific-related materials.

28. Later writers have uncovered some of this history. See, for example: *New Zealand Letters of Thomas Arnold the Younger,* ed. James Bertram (Auckland: University of Auckland and Oxford University Press, 1966), ISBN 0196479800; *Mary Taylor, Friend of Charlotte Bronte. Letters from New Zealand and Elsewhere,* ed. with narrative and notes by Joan Stevens (Auckland: Auckland University Press and Oxford University Press, 1972), ISBN 0196476232; Eric Hall McCormick, *The Friend of John Keats: A Life of Charles Armitage Brown* (Auckland: Auckland University Press, 1989), ISBN 0864730810. Similarly, the diaries of many early travelers have been edited and reissued.

29. See the introductory chapters of *The Penguin History of New Zealand Literature* by Patrick Evans (Auckland: Penguin, 1990), ISBN 0140113711.

30. A useful guide is *Art Galleries and Museums of New Zealand* by Keith W. Thompson (Wellington: Reed, 1981), ISBN 0589103645, which provides descriptions and addresses.

31. Dennis McEldowney, cited above, provides an excellent summary of this sometimes chaotic history, and Iris Winchester, *New Zealand Periodicals of Literary Interest* (Wellington: National Library Service, 1962) provides a useful guide to publications before that date.

32. Two articles, now somewhat old, by D. S. Long, "The Publication of Contemporary New Zealand Literature," in *NZL* 37, no. 6 (1974): 290–97, and 39, no. 1 (1976): 18–22, provide a good overview of local publishing.
33. Heather Roberts in *Where Did She Come From? New Zealand Women Novelists 1982–1987* (Wellington: Allen and Unwin, 1989) has provided an initial foray into this history.
34. I. R. Willison, "Australian and New Zealand Studies: The Development of a Bibliographic Infrastructure," *NZL* 44, no. 6 (1984): 93–98.
35. Austin Graham Bagnall, "Reflections on Some Unfinished Business: The Retrospective National Bibliography, 1946–1976," *NZL* 40, no. 2 (1977): 40–50.

Editors and Contributors

GAYLE GARLOCK has over twenty years' working experience in collection management in Canadian research libraries. He also teaches courses in collection management, is on the board of directors of the Canadian Institute of Historical Microreproductions, and co-chaired the first Canadian Collections Management Institute.

CECILY JOHNS has been deputy director of University Libraries at the University of California, Santa Barbara, since 1985. Before that she was associate university librarian for Collections and Information Services at the University of Cincinnati. While at Cincinnati, she chaired the Collection Management and Development Committee of RTSD (now ALCTS) and organized the Cincinnati Collection Management and Development Institute.

MURRAY S. MARTIN is professor of library science emeritus from Tufts University. He was born and educated in New Zealand and has worked in libraries in three countries, including thirteen years at the Pennsylvania State University, where he helped found the New Zealand collection. He is now a consultant and contributes papers and presentations on New Zealand literature as well as library science.

WILLIAM Z. SCHENCK is collections program officer in the Collections Policy Office of the Library of Congress. He has worked in collection development and acquisitions positions at Yale, the University of North Carolina at Chapel Hill, and the University of Oregon. He founded the Australian Studies Discussion Group in ACRL/ALA and has been active in ALCTS.

Index

DATE DUE

GAYLORD   PRINTED IN U.S.A.